Olaf's Kitchen

Olaf's Kitchen

A Master Chef Shares His Passion

OLAF MERTENS

John Wiley & Sons Canada, Ltd.

Library and Archives Canada Cataloguing in Publication Data

Library and Archives Canada Cataloguing in Publication Data

Mertens, Olaf
     Olaf's kitchen : a master chef shares his passion / Olaf Mertens.

Includes index.
ISBN 978-0-470-15566-0 (bound).—ISBN 978-0-470-15565-3 (pbk.)

     1. Cookery. I. Title.
TX714.M467 2008   641.5   C2008-900608-9

Production Credits
Cover and interior design: Ian Koo
Typesetting: Natalia Burobina
Interior photo-imaging: Jason Vandenberg
Front cover photo: Satravath Pradalokaew
Back cover photo: Morgan Whibley
Interior photography: Satravath Pradalokaew (colour photos); Morgan Whibley (black and white photos)
Printer: Quebecor World—Taunton

John Wiley & Sons Canada, Ltd.
6045 Freemont Blvd.
Mississauga, Ontario
L5R 4J3

Printed in the United States

1 2 3 4 5 QW 12 11 10 09 08

To my lovely wife and best friend: Jennifer, a.k.a. my food critic.

To the greatest boys any dad could have: Nicolas, Taylor, and Owen. Will one of you please consider becoming a chef?

To the rest of my family: You are a component without which all of this would not be nearly as good a journey.

I come from generations of foodies whose talents range from being a German cook in eighteenth-century English manors to running a small, local butcher shop in the west end of Toronto during the Depression. It is through these past generations that food and cooking have become part of my roots.

I cook because food is, and always has been, an integral part of my being. It's what brings my family and friends together around the table to share the day's events, tell stories, laugh, and live life. For me, food is the real magic of life.

Contents

Thank you to...

Donna, my "ghost writer," who for many years has made my recipes make sense. Many thanks.

To my family, Mom, Marcus, Gary, Marty, Alison, Louise, Chris, Leah, Jade, Hannah, the Mertens family, the Urquhart clan, the Whiteheads, the Whibleys, the Tischmeiers, the Pfaffs, and Haussner families.

To my partner Brian, for his friendship and all the years of support and teaching me to enjoy the journey.

To Christiane Cote and Leah Marie Fairbank, and the entire Wiley Publishing team that has made this dream come true.

To Rob, who has worked and supported me for so long. Mark, my friend and partner, as well as the entire HIP Restaurants family—all the chefs, cooks, pastry chefs, servers, bartenders, dishwashers, cleaners, and especially to the patrons who come to our restaurants.

The Book Makers: the photographers, Morgan Whibley and Max Satravath Pradalokaew (via Thailand)—your creativity and talents show in each and every photo. You put my visions into pictures.

My team of chefs: "Desi" Desiree, Nic, Patrick, Alex, "Gorbi" Misha, Christine, Arthur, Luther, Ali, Jonathan, Jackie, Trevor, Andrew, and Logan. Each of you makes me a better chef.

My colleagues and friends: Michelin Man Bernd Siener, Ted Reader, Michael and Anna Olson, John Sleeman, Brad Long, and Manny Tsouvallas. For years we've kept an eye on each other. Lucky for all of us.

To the farmers, local food suppliers, Sean Kelly and the food makers—what would my plates look like without your expertise and working the land to give us the best, right in our backyard?

To all the kitchen stewards for keeping our kitchens spotless. This is just a bit of recognition, but you deserve so much more.

I would like to thank my friends and anyone I may have forgotten that enjoyed the culinary journey with me. It's not over yet.

Englische Speise

Herzen braten: Die Herzen werden mit Speck umwickelt, und ins heiße Fett legen.

Printed letterhead on the loose sheet:

J. HERMANN,
ST. VEDAST,
HIGH ROAD,
WHETSTONE,
LONDON, N.

Introduction

My entire life I knew I was going to be a chef. The power that food has to bring people together around a common table to enjoy stories, laughs, and great meals has always been revered in my family. It is one of the most important bonds of life.

I have been cooking for some twenty years now, not only as a chef but also as one of many in a long line of cooks. I thought I knew about all the culinary talents of my heritage until recently, when I found out that my great grand-aunt was a cook in some of Germany's and England's great manors. Her name was Martha Tischmeier and she was born in northeast Germany. I was very fortunate to be given her spectacularly hand-scripted cooking journal that dates back to the late 1800s and early 1900s. It is this journal that has inspired me to tell the story of my history and unique look upon, and approach to, German cuisine. This book is the journey of my life told through food and family.

Let's start at the beginning. I was born in Berlin, Germany, and immigrated to Canada at two years of age. It was my parents' wish that I maintain both the language and culture of Germany, so I attended German school on weekends and celebrated all the various German customs while growing up. Our family opened a German food shop where we offered typical German delicacies, magazines, and homemade goodies. Throughout grade school I was lucky enough to spend most of my summers with my grandparents and aunts. It is during these visits that I watched and learned the great secrets of their regional cooking. When I was a youngster, German ways were all around me. At the same time, I was learning the life of a Canadian boy. As an adult looking back I am aware of what a wonderful thing it was to have been able to enjoy the best of both worlds. It is in keeping with these two worlds that I have been able to develop my individuality and signature foods.

As a teenager nearing the end of high school in a suburb of Toronto, Canada, I made the decision to pursue my childhood dream of becoming a chef. I knew from my upbringing that the educational system in Germany, in particular the culinary trade, was far superior to the one in Canada. Picking up and moving to Berlin on my own when most of my friends were heading off to party at college and university didn't initially seem like a big deal. I remember that time in my life with so many emotions and now truly understand the phrase "it was the best of times, it was the worst of times."

Working as an eighteen-year-old apprentice in Berlin during the mid 1980s took me from cooking in Europe's top luxury hotels and fine dining restaurants to grabbing a snack at the local butcher shop or an *imbiss sausage* after a late-night bar crawl. These great food memories always remind me to cook deliciously, or to *immer lecker kochen*, as we say in German.

In the mid to late eighties, European cuisine, and more specifically German cuisine, was moving from the traditional service of big, hearty food portions to the more refined and artful presentations of nouvelle cuisine. It was an exceptional time to be in a one–Michelin star kitchen watching and learning while such an important movement took over the way food was cooked and served.

This unique opportunity was further enhanced when, in 1987, I experienced Germany's 750th birthday party. Almost every night in our hotel there was a celebration of some kind to mark the monumental occasion. It was at these events that I truly learned how to be a buffet, banquet, and gala dinner specialist. It was overwhelming for my chef to have to come up with the new and innovative creations that would make each event a bit better than the last. I was a part of every celebration and wrote down every dish served. Talk about being at the right place at the right time in history. To make it even more significant, Germany was still a divided country, and Berlin was very much a divided city. The opportunity to take part in the celebration as a cook in what was then East Berlin was a fantastic part of that year.

Those were some of the hardest, yet some of the most fantastic, years of my life. They are the roots of some of my favorite food recipes and definitely my favorite food stories. Now that I am back at home in Canada, I use the classic German techniques I learned and combine them with the world's best ingredients, most of which are here in the southern Ontario region that is my backyard.

In the following chapters you will travel with me to Germany, Bavaria, Austria, and then finally back to Canada and the family table that I so dearly treasure. Each trip has been a culinary adventure that has taken my cuisine to new heights. The recipes in this book represent my year of apprenticeship in the grand hotels of Berlin, my tough and demanding schedule in the Steigenberger Hotels, and the Master Chef course that proved to be a great maturing and very humbling experience. I spent months of study immersed in the history of cuisine development and discussions and arguments about culinary theory.

All of my trips abroad have inevitably brought me back to my home in southern Ontario, where I have all the fresh, quality ingredients I could ask for. I have an abundance of wonderful produce, meats, fish, and other food treasures in this part of the world. Ontario white asparagus and strawberries, Muskoka wild blueberries, Holland Marsh fresh vegetables, Caledon's selection of potatoes and wild mushrooms and, of course, Niagara region fruits, flowers, and probably the best selection of wines in the world. All of these are but a few of the delights at my fingertips.

Let me show you how I marry my cultures and the roots of my cooking with the passion and pride of being in my own kitchen. My unique style brings a heritage of German cuisine together with contemporary Canadian flair. These are the dishes that people have been talking about. Try them out and come along for a ride.

I hope you enjoy the journey.

Olaf

Standards

All recipes are prepared for **4 portions** unless otherwise indicated.

All ingredients should be fresh and in prime condition, preferably organic, and even better if locally grown.

All ingredients need to be cleaned, washed, and stored properly until you are ready to start cooking.

All herbs are fresh.

Since most spices only last for six months in your cupboard, buy fresh and grind them yourself in a coffee grinder or pestle.

Pepper is always freshly ground, be it white or black.

Chicken or beef broths will give true flavors when purchased as low-sodium or salt-free—then you can control the salt!

All eggs are large, preferably organic for optimum flavor, and room temperature.

Do not refrigerate tomatoes, and use vine-ripened for ultimate flavor.

White bread crumbs refers to crust-less, day-old white bread, ground into crumbs.

Some cheeses (like Parmesan), lemon, or orange zest are best achieved using a rasp—the kitchen's best friend!

Salt is sea salt, unless otherwise indicated.

Greetings from the Kitchen

Greetings from the Kitchen

Greusse aus die Kuche! "Greetings from the kitchen" is a phrase borrowed

from the executive chef I worked under in Berlin. I remember the first time

I heard him use it; he was welcoming a newly seated table of diners by

personally delivering the customary bite-size introduction to multicourse

menus. I was struck by the chef's attentiveness and how it immediately

put guests at ease while simultaneously giving them a hint of what the

kitchen had to offer. So, now, every chance I get I like to personally greet

my guests and welcome them with the echo of my mentor's words and

one of my own small palate teasers. Here are a few of my favorite one- or

two-bite first-course offerings.

First Bites

First Bites

Tomato Salad Shooters

Hot summer nights are the perfect time to enjoy the first tomatoes of the season. These infused vodka shots and the tomato salad skewers are a fun way to start a festive evening. Be sure to make extra skewers because everyone is guaranteed to want more than one shot.

Tomato Salad Shooters

Tomato-Infused Vodka

10 large vine-ripened tomatoes, very overripe
4 oz. vodka
5 basil leaves
1 tsp. herbal vinegar
1 1/2 tbsp. orange juice, or the juice from half an orange
1 tsp. orange zest, or the zest from half an orange
1 tbsp. sugar
1 tsp. sea salt
1 clove garlic
dash cayenne pepper to taste

Place all ingredients in a food processor and blend until tomatoes are coarsely chopped. Strain the mixture into a bowl through three layers of cheesecloth then gather the corners of the cloths together and tie them with string so that all the pulp is gathered in a pouch. Secure the pouch so it dangles from a refrigerator shelf and can drip into a bowl beneath. Leave to drip overnight.

Tomato Salad Skewers

1 piece Buffalo mozzarella
1/4 cup olive oil
sea salt
pepper
8 skewers or swizzle sticks
8 vine-ripened cherry tomatoes
8 shooter glasses, chilled
8 sprigs oregano

Tear the cheese into small cubes. Toss with olive oil, salt, and pepper.

Make garnishes for the shots by layering tips of the skewers with a cheese cube, a basil leaf, and a tomato.

Pour the infused vodka evenly into chilled shooter glasses, drop in a sprig of oregano, and garnish with a salad skewer.

For a bit of a twist, use test tubes instead of shooter glasses. The test tubes can be stood up in cucumber slices that have been hollowed out with a melon baller.

. . . .

Tip: Small bits of pulp may leak through the cheesecloth as the last of the vodka drips though. Pour the vodka into the shooter glasses slowly and carefully to avoid disturbing any sediment that may have formed at the bottom of the bowl. This will produce nice clear-looking shots.

. . . .

Tomato Melon Salad
with Strawberries and Olive Dust

Strawberries and Olive Dust

1 pint strawberries, halved
1 tbsp. sugar
salt and pepper
1/4 cup olive oil
1 cup calamata olives, pitted

Preheat oven to 250°F.

Toss the strawberry pieces in the sugar, salt, pepper, and olive oil, spread them out on a baking sheet lined with parchment paper, and oven-dry for 20 minutes. Set aside to cool.

Spread the olives on a separate parchment paper–lined baking sheet and oven-dry for 2 hours, or until the olives are hard. Set aside to cool.

Once cooled, chop the olives into fine crumbs.

Tomato Melon Salad

8 oz. watermelon, cut into pieces
2 oz. ouzo
1 cucumber, sliced
2 pints vine-ripened grape tomatoes
1 pint figs, sliced
1 bunch radish sprouts
1 head Boston bibb lettuce
4 oz. feta cheese, crumbled
2 tsp. lemon zest, or the zest from 1 lemon
1/2 cup chopped oregano
1/2 cup sliced basil
1/2 cup sliced mint
sea salt
ground pepper

Toss the watermelon and ouzo in a small dish and set aside to soak for 30 minutes. Combine all remaining salad ingredients, including the strawberries and the Olive Dust, and portion into four individual bowls. Dress with Red Wine Vinaigrette (page 207) just prior to serving.

Tomato Melon Salad with Strawberries and Olive Dust

I love working with fruits and vegetables! Especially tomatoes—they are so versatile. The addition of feta, strawberries, and Olive Dust to this dish makes each mouthful an explosion of flavors.

Potato Crisps
with Herbed Feta Dip

Recent travels to Greece have left me duly inspired. Homemade olive-oil potato chips and a fantastic feta cheese dip. What more can you ask for? As they say in Greece: *Yamass!*

Potato Crisps

1 russet potato
1 yellow-flesh potato
1 sweet potato
1 purple potato
3 tbsp. lemon juice, or the juice from 1 lemon
1 quart olive oil, or enough to make about 3 inches in a
    heavy-bottomed pot
sea salt

Slice the potatoes on the thinnest setting of a mandolin and soak in a bowl of cold water and lemon juice for one hour.

Carefully heat a large pot of olive oil to 275°F. Line a baking sheet with parchment paper and paper towel; place nearby, with a slotted spoon or mesh ladle. Completely dry the potato slices and begin frying in small batches until golden brown and crispy. Drain on the prepared baking sheet and, while still warm, season with sea salt. Keep warm.

Herbed Feta Dip

2 cups feta cheese, crumbled
1 cup yogurt
 sea salt
 cracked black pepper
1/4 cup parsley, finely sliced
1/4 cup basil, finely sliced
1/4 cup oregano, finely chopped
6 tbsp. lemon juice, or the juice from 2 lemons
4 tsp. lemon zest, or the zest from 2 lemons
1/2 cup olive oil

Combine all ingredients except the olive oil in a bowl and whisk.

Slowly drizzle in the olive oil so that the mixture emulsifies to a thick, dressing-like consistency. Adjust salt and pepper to taste.

. . . .

Tip: The sugar content of the sweet potatoes will cause them to brown faster than the other potatoes. It's better to cook them separately so that they do not burn.

. . . .

Oh, asparagus! Because of its stringy skin and light, bitter taste, white asparagus is slightly more challenging to prepare than its green counterpart. Here is a simple way to blanch it, followed by three great ways to use it. Try one or try them all—you won't be disappointed!

White Asparagus Three Ways

2 lbs. white asparagus
12 cups water
1 cup sugar
1/2 cup salt
6 tbsp. orange juice, or the juice from 2 oranges
3 tbsp. lemon juice, or the juice from 1 lemon
1 bay leaf

Remove outer layer from all the asparagus stalks with a vegetable peeler and cut approximately one inch off the bottoms.

In a large pot, bring the water to a rolling boil and add the remaining ingredients. Add the asparagus and blanch for 3 minutes or until tender when poked with a knife. Transfer the asparagus to an ice bath and allow to cool. Reserve the cooking broth.

. . . .

Tip: To make a fine, quick soup, add the asparagus ends and peelings to the leftover cooking broth. Simmer, season to taste with salt and pepper, then purée.

. . . .

Roasted Espresso Balsamic Paint

1 cup sugar
1 cup balsamic vinegar
1/2 cup espresso or instant espresso powder
1 tsp. salt
1/2 tsp. white pepper
1/3 blanched asparagus

Preheat oven to 350°F.

Combine the sugar and balsamic vinegar in a small pot and simmer over medium heat for 10 minutes. Add the coffee and simmer for another 3 minutes. Season with salt and pepper.

Place the asparagus in a shallow baking dish, cover with half the espresso balsamic paint, and bake for 5 minutes. Use the remaining paint as a dip when serving.

Sweet and Sour Asparagus

1/2 cup sugar
1/2 cup herb-flavored vinegar
1 cup asparagus cooking water
1/3 blanched asparagus
1/2 cup carrots, finely diced
1/2 cup celery, finely diced
1/2 cup red and yellow peppers, finely diced
1/4 cup chives, sliced
1/4 cup thyme, chopped, for garnish

Combine sugar and vinegar in a small pot and simmer over medium heat until reduced by half; the mixture should have a syrup-like consistency. Add asparagus cooking water and simmer for an additional 5 minutes. Place asparagus in a flat glass dish; add carrots, celery, and peppers. Pour broth over vegetables, cover, and let marinate in the refrigerator for at least 24 hours. Garnish with sliced chives and thyme just before serving.

Asparagus "Frites" with Herb Sauce

2 cups flour
2 egg whites, whisked
1 cup Parmesan cheese, grated
2 cups fresh bread crumbs
1/3 blanched asparagus
 olive oil

Use the three-bowl method: put the flour in one dish, the egg whites in a second dish, and toss the cheese and bread crumbs together in a third dish.

Dredge all but the tips of the asparagus spears in the flour, then dip into the egg whites, and finally coat with the cheese and bread crumb mixture. Line a baking sheet with parchment paper. Place coated asparagus on the baking sheet, then refrigerate for 15 minutes.

In a large frying pan, over medium heat, bring about an inch of olive oil to 275°F. Fry asparagus spears until golden brown, then carefully remove from the pan using a slotted spoon or tongs and place on a tray lined with paper towel to drain excess oil.

Herb Sauce

1 cup sour cream
1/4 cup onion, finely diced
1/4 cup chives, finely chopped
1 1/2 tbsp. lemon juice, or the juice from half a lemon
 salt and pepper to taste

Combine all the ingredients and put into a small dish for dipping. This sauce can be made ahead of time and set aside.

Curing salmon was one of the things I had to attempt while working in Berlin. I have played with many variations, and years of experience have finally led me to this winning recipe. If you are not familiar with herbal schnapps just ask your local liquor store retailer to help you find it.

Herbal Schnapps—Cured Salmon Sticks

Herbal Schnapps-Cured Salmon Sticks

1 lb. wild salmon, boneless, skin on
1 bunch dill, chopped
2 tbsp. green peppercorns
1 tsp. sea salt
1/4 cup salt
1/4 cup brown sugar
3 tbsp. orange juice, or the juice from 1 orange
2 tsp. orange zest, or the zest from 1 orange
8 oz. herbal schnapps

Place the salmon skin side down on a 12" x 12" square of tin foil.

Sprinkle with chopped dill, peppercorns, salts, brown sugar, orange juice, and zest.

Fold the sides of the foil up to create a small lip, then pour in the schnapps. Fold the foil around the salmon and crimp the edges to make an airtight parcel. Place the salmon between two trays or plates and let it rest under something heavy for 12 hours.

To serve, wash off the salmon and cut it into very thin slices. Weave the slices onto wooden skewers and arrange them on a platter. Serve with Herbed Mustard Dip.

. . . .

Tip: As you begin to feel more comfortable with the process of curing, feel free to invent your own brines by experimenting with different spirits, herbs, and citrus fruits.

. . . .

Herbed Mustard Dip

1/2 cup Dijon mustard
1/2 cup herbal schnapps
1 tsp. brown sugar
1 tbsp. honey
1 1/2 tbsp. lemon juice, or the juice of half a lemon
salt and pepper to taste

Combine all ingredients and put into a bowl small enough to sit amongst the salmon skewers.

Fancy Fish and Chips

This is fish and chips taken to the next level. Moist strips of fish woven through potatoes and fried until perfectly crisp make for one-bite wonders.

2 large yellow or russet potatoes, peeled
3 tbsp. lemon juice, or the juice from 1 lemon
6 smelts, cleaned
7 oz. Tilapia filets
7 oz. salmon
4 cups olive oil, for frying
sea salt
white pepper
1/2 cup dill, sliced
1/4 cup chives, sliced

Cut the potatoes lengthwise in 1/8-inch slices, like a thick potato chip. Cut short slits in the slices at one-inch intervals, making sure you leave the potato uncut at the top, bottom, and sides. You will use the slits when you weave the fish filets through the potatoes. Fill a dish with cold water, stir in the lemon juice, and add potato slices. Set aside.

Cut all the fish into 1/4" x 2" pieces. Dry potato slices, then weave the fish strips through the cuts in the slices.

In a medium pot over medium heat, heat the olive oil to 275°F. Gently deep fry until the potato and fish are golden brown.

Remove from oil using a slotted spoon, place in a dish lined with paper towels, and immediately season with salt and pepper. Mound chips onto a plate and sprinkle with dill and chives.

Dip

2 cloves garlic
1 1/2 cups mayonnaise
1/2 cup sour cream
3 tbsp. lemon juice, or the juice from 1 lemon
2 tsp. lemon zest, or the zest from 1 lemon
salt and pepper to taste
1/2 cup capers, chopped
1/4 cup chives, finely sliced
1/4 cup parsley, finely sliced

Combine all the ingredients, cover, and refrigerate until ready to use.

. . . .

Tip: These chips are best served as soon as they are ready. If they sit after being cooked, they may become soggy.

. . . .

Duck Empanadas with Salsa Verde

I have always been enthralled with Spanish food, and handmade pastry filled with big flavors is just about the best thing any party can serve up!

Pastry

3 3/4 cups flour
1 tbsp. corn starch
1 tsp. salt
1 egg, beaten
1/3 cup unsalted butter, melted
1 1/2 cups cold water
1 tsp. olive oil

On a flat surface, mix flour, cornstarch, and salt together using your fingers. Hollow out the center and pour in all the wet ingredients. Gradually mix the flour into the wet ingredients until soft dough forms. Place dough in a dish, cover, and refrigerate for at least one hour.

Filling

1 small onion, minced
1 tbsp. olive oil
1 lb. braised duck meat (page 91), or store-bought BBQ
    duck, diced
1/3 cup chicken stock
3 tbsp. orange juice, or the juice from 1 orange
2 tsp. orange zest, or the zest from 1 orange
1/4 cup parsley, sliced
3/4 cup white bread crumbs
salt and pepper to taste

Egg Wash

1 egg
1/4 cup milk

Preheat oven to 350°F.

In a frying pan over medium heat, sauté the onion in olive oil until translucent. Add the remaining ingredients and mix.

On a lightly floured surface, roll out the chilled dough to about 1/8-inch thickness, then cut into 3- or 4-inch rounds using a cookie cutter. You should have about 24 cirlces of dough. In a small bowl, whisk together egg and milk. Brush the edges of each circle with egg wash. This will help seal the pastry after it's folded.

Place a heaping tablespoon of filling in the center of each circle. Fold the sides up to form crescents, and seal the edges by pinching them together. Place empanadas on a baking sheet lined with parchment paper, brush tops with remaining egg wash, and bake for 15 minutes, or until golden brown.
Serve with Salsa Verde.

Salsa Verde

1 cup cilantro
1/2 cup parsley
1/2 cup scallions
1/4 cup onion
1/4 cup jalapeño pepper
1 clove garlic
3/4 cup extra-virgin olive oil
2 tbsp. lime juice, or the juice of 1 lime
salt and pepper to taste

Place all ingredients except olive oil, lime juice, salt, and pepper on a cutting board, chop coarsely, then put into a serving bowl. Drizzle with the olive oil and lime juice. Adjust salt and pepper to taste.

• •

Tip: The roasted duck is only one possibility amongst an endless variety of fillings. Get creative with things like mushrooms, spinach, cheese, beef, or chorizo. Whatever you choose to experiment with, remember to keep your filling mixtures as moist as possible.

• •

Mini Duck Burgers

Mini Duck Burgers

I first came up with the idea for these burgers while working in Berlin in the mid '80s. The idea has always stuck with me, and the recipe is now one of my signature dishes. I serve these little burgers at catered events, cocktail parties, and as a healthy snack. One of the fun things about this recipe is that it replaces traditional condiments, such as pickles, tomato, lettuce, and mustard, with ingredients that complement the duck.

Patties

1 lb. braised duck meat (page 191), or store-bought
   cooked duck, finely diced
1/2 cup leeks, finely sliced
1/2 cup onion, minced
2 tsp. orange zest, or the zest from 1 orange
1 tbsp. sage, sliced
1 tbsp. parsley, sliced
2 egg yolks, beaten
1/3 cup fresh bread crumbs
salt and pepper to taste

Burger Assembly

8 whole wheat muesli buns, split
1 pint alfalfa sprouts
1 pint figs, sliced
1 orange, peeled and cut into slices
2 tsp. orange zest, or the zest from 1 orange
1/4 cup orange marmalade, store-bought

Preheat the oven to 250°F.

In a large bowl, combine patty ingredients and season with salt and pepper. Form into 2-inch patties and place on a baking sheet lined with parchment paper. Bake for 10 minutes.

While the patties are baking, toast the buns and prepare to build your mini burgers. Toss the orange zest with the sprouts and layer onto the top half of the bun with the fig and orange slices. Spread the other half of the bun with marmalade, then top it with the duck.

• •

Tip: Warming the patties slowly at a low temperature allows for the duck meat to remain moist and tender.

• •

Fresh from the Earth

Fresh from the Earth

Give me real vegetables! All the better if they're fresh from the ground and still coated with the rich, dark soil they grew in. Fresh, organic garden vegetables taste like nothing else. The recipes that follow stand out because they are made to accent the distinct, natural flavors of the vegetables they incorporate. Although I am a self-avowed meat and potatoes man, I could survive on these recipes alone if I had to. From comforting soups to savory dishes, all of these recipes can easily be served as the main component of a meal.

Wholesome Vegetable Cooking

Wholesome Vegetable Cooking

Butternut Squash Soup with Muesli Popcorn Clusters

Autumn: colored leaves, cool days, and cold nights. This soup is perfect for when you've returned from a brisk walk. The muesli clusters add a healthy crunch, and the last-minute addition of freshly juiced vegetables gives a little extra punch to the base flavors of the soup.

Butternut Squash Soup with Muesli Popcorn Clusters

Butternut Squash Soup

1/4 cup olive oil
3 small to medium butternut squash
4 medium carrots
1 medium onion, diced
1 tsp. ginger root, grated
1/2 tsp. allspice
1 tbsp. curry powder
1 stick cinnamon
1 bay leaf
salt and white pepper to taste
10 cups vegetable stock
1/2 cup buckwheat honey
1 cup dried apricots, diced
Muesli Popcorn Clusters (recipe follows)
1/4 cup chervil, coarsely chopped

Peel, seed, and cube the squash; peel and dice the carrots. Add oil to a stockpot and place over medium heat; add 2/3 of the squash and 1/2 of the carrots; then add onion, ginger, allspice, curry powder, cinnamon stick, and bay leaf. Sauté until all the vegetables are soft, then season with salt and pepper. Add the stock, honey, and diced apricot. Simmer for 30 minutes.

Remove the cinnamon stick and bay leaf; pour contents of stockpot into a blender or food processor and purée. Be careful: this liquid is hot! Strain purée through a fine sieve. Adjust seasonings.

Juice or purée the reserved raw carrot and squash.

Whisk the raw vegetables into the hot soup, then ladle the soup into warm bowls, float a Muesli Popcorn Cluster in the center of each, and garnish with chervil.

. . . .

Tip: Fresh juice added at the last minute to an already flavorful soup punches up the key flavor profile.

. . . .

Muesli Popcorn Clusters

4 cups marshmallows (mini, or large ones cut into quarters)
2 cups oat muesli cereal blend
1/2 cup crushed cornflakes
3/4 cup your choice of dried fruits (raisins, mango, cranberries)
1 cup toasted mixed nuts or seeds
4 cups popped popcorn

Preheat the oven to 200°F.

In a large pan, over medium heat, melt the marshmallows, stirring constantly.

In a large bowl, toss muesli, cornflakes, dried fruit, and nuts. Set aside approximately a quarter of this mixture. Add the popcorn; mix it in, then carefully stir in melted marshmallow. Cool until comfortable enough to handle. Divide into eight sections. Using your hands, form into balls. Roll balls in the mixture you set aside, then place on a baking tray lined with parchment paper. Bake for 5 minutes or until firm.

Serve immediately with the soup, or make ahead and store in an airtight container.

. . . .

Tip: Served on their own, these clusters make a great treat.

. . . .

White Asparagus Soup with Root Vegetable Crisps

This soup is inspired by Michelin Star Chef Bernie Siener. The white asparagus purée is accented by small root vegetable crisps to make a sophisticated play on breakfast cereal. After all, grown-ups should have fun too!

White Asparagus Soup

2 lbs. white asparagus
1/4 cup unsalted butter
1 medium onion, diced
1 large yellow-flesh potato, diced
1/4 cup flour
6 cups chicken or vegetable stock
1 bay leaf
3 tbsp. lemon juice, or the juice from 1 large lemon
1/3 cup orange juice, or the juice from 2 medium oranges
1 cup whipping cream, warmed
1/4 tsp. nutmeg
salt and white pepper to taste

Remove asparagus tips and set aside for use in Root Vegetable Crisps. Dice asparagus stalks. In a stockpot on medium high, melt the butter, then sauté the onion, asparagus pieces, and potato for 5 minutes. Do not let the vegetables brown. Dust with flour and mix well. Whisk in the stock, add the bay leaf, and stir constantly so the flour doesn't burn or stick to the bottom of the pot. Add the lemon and orange juice. Simmer for 30 minutes.

White Asparagus Soup with Root Vegetable Crisps

In a separate pot, warm the cream.

Remove bay leaf from the stockpot. Add the cream and nutmeg. Stirring constantly, continue to simmer for approximately 5 minutes. Season with salt and pepper.

Purée, then strain through a fine sieve.

Root Vegetable Crisps

1 small red-skin potato
1 small gold-flesh potato
1 small purple-flesh potato
1 small parsnip
1 small carrot
1 small sweet potato
1 small beet
olive oil, for frying
salt and pepper to taste
1 box pea sprouts
1/2 lb. green and white asparagus tips

Use as many or as few of the suggested vegetables as you like. Peel and slice on the thinnest setting of a mandolin. Place slices in ice-cold water to remove some of the starch and prevent them from drying out.

Heat the oil to 310°F and slowly fry the vegetable slices in small batches for approximately one minute, or until golden brown and crispy. Remove with a slotted spoon and place on paper towel to absorb any excess oil. Season with salt and pepper while still warm.

Steam the asparagus tips until just tender. Set aside.

To serve: Sprinkle bowls with the root vegetable chips, fill with soup, then top with sprouts and steamed asparagus tips. Or allow your guests to pour the soup themselves from a large teapot or several individual pots. Be sure to warm the teapots so the soup stays nice and hot.

• •

Tip: Cold cream does not react well to hot liquids. Warming the cream allows the two to combine without any curdling. Enhance the flavor of this soup by making it ahead of time and chilling it overnight. The tastes will marry together and become more integrated.

• •

A mandolin is a great kitchen tool. There is nothing else like it for slicing vegetables paper-thin.

To make the potatoes extra crispy, soak the slices in cold water with a squeeze of lemon juice added to it.

Sauerkraut Crème Soup

Served hot or cold, sauerkraut is great all on its own. Add a little

cream and a few special ingredients, and you end up with love

on a spoon.

1/4 cup vegetable oil
1 medium onions, diced
1 medium apple, grated
1 medium yellow-flesh potato, peeled and diced
2 cups dry white wine
1/3 cup flour
4 cups sauerkraut, with liquid
2 bay leaves
4 cups Vegetable Stock (page 182)
nutmeg
salt
pepper
1 cup whipping cream
1/4 tsp. ground caraway seeds
1 cup apple cider
2 tbsp. lemon juice, or the juice from 1 medium lemon
2 cups white cabbage juice, store bought
pumpernickel bread croutons

In a large stockpot, over medium-high heat, add the oil and sauté the onion, apple, and potato for a few minutes. Add the white wine and reduce by half. Whisk in the flour until you have a smooth paste.

Add the sauerkraut, bay leaves, and vegetable stock. Reduce heat to medium. Season to taste with nutmeg, salt, and pepper.

In a separate pot, or in the microwave, warm the cream then add to the soup. Simmer for 30 minutes.

Remove bay leaves. Purée the soup, then pass it through a fine sieve. Add the caraway. Just before serving, add apple cider, lemon, and cabbage juice to give the soup a little extra kick. Garnish with croutons.

Sweet and Sour
Spice-Infused Tomatoes

Tomatoes are just great as is, yet they can be used in so many

different ways. This infusion turns each little tomato into a bite

that will zip across your tongue and perk up your whole palate.

4 cups water
3 cups sugar
2 cups white vinegar
1 small red chili pepper
3 tbsp. orange juice and zest, or the juice and zest
   of 1 orange
1 vanilla bean, marrow scraped
1/2 cup basil leaves
3 bay leaves
3 star anise
1 tbsp. coriander seed
1 tsp. fennel seed
1/2 tsp. cracked white peppercorns
24 vine-ripened cherry tomatoes

In a large pot over medium high heat, simmer all ingredients, except the tomatoes, for 10 minutes.

Place the tomatoes in a large dish that is deep enough for them to be completely submerged. Pour in the infusing liquid, cover, and refrigerate for 24 hours, or overnight at the very least.

. . . .

Tip: Leaving the tomatoes on the vine makes for a more appealing presentation. The vanilla bean can be saved for future recipes: cover it with salt or sugar and seal it in an airtight container.

. . . .

Confit Vegetable Parcel

Confit Vegetable Parcel with Goat Cheese Dip

Here I take my lead from Italian chefs. Citrus-seasoned vegetables sealed in crispy flatbread combine two of Italy's finest staples.

Confit Vegetable Parcel

1 Flatbread (page 198)
1 cup olive oil
1/2 tsp. sugar
1/2 tsp. salt
1 tsp. black peppercorns
4 medium vine-ripened tomatoes, halved
1 bulb fennel, sliced lengthwise into 1/2-inch widths
1 large eggplant cut into 1/2-inch slices
1 small red onion, quartered
4 garlic cloves, whole
2 peppers, seeded, cut into thick strips
1 tbsp. rosemary, chopped
1 tbsp. basil, chopped
1 tbsp. thyme, chopped
1 medium zucchini, chopped
2 tsp. lemon zest, or the zest from 1 lemon

Preheat the oven to 350°F.

Prepare flatbread dough; set aside.

Mix all remaining ingredients until vegetables are coated. Spread out in an earthenware dish and bake for 15 minutes, or until vegetables are cooked.

Remove dish from oven and let it cool slightly.

Roll out the flatbread dough and wrap it around the top of the earthenware dish.

Return dish to the oven and bake for 15 minutes, or until bread is golden brown.

Goat Cheese Dip

1 cup goat cheese
3 cups plain yogurt
3 tbsp. lemon juice, or the juice from 1 lemon
1/4 cup olive oil
salt and pepper to taste

Combine all ingredients and pour into a small dish for dipping.

. . . .

Tip: You can bake the vegetables one day in advance then wrap them in the flatbread and bake them just before serving.

. . . .

Scalloped Kohlrabi

My family loves the mild, broccoli-like flavor of kohlrabi. Unfortunately, this fantastic vegetable is highly underused. My recipe is an attempt at getting people to fall in love with this lonely little vegetable.

4 bulbs kohlrabi
1 tsp. unsalted butter
1 tsp. flour
1 tsp. honey
1/2 tsp. apple cider vinegar
1 cup kohlrabi broth, from cooking water
1 egg yolk, beaten
1/2 cup sour cream
salt and pepper to taste
4 red radishes, cut into 1/8-inch slices
1 large baking apple, skin on, cut into 1/8-inch slices

Preheat the oven to 250°F

Grease an earthenware dish and set aside.

Fill a large pot with salted water—make sure there is enough water to cover the kohlrabi completely. Bring the water to a boil.

Remove top leaves from the kohlrabi and peel. Boil the bulbs until tender, about 15 minutes, then drain (save the liquid) and cool.

Cut the kohlrabi into quarter-inch slices.

In a large pan, over medium heat, melt the butter then add the flour, stirring constantly until a smooth paste forms. Add the honey, apple cider vinegar, and kohlrabi broth, simmer for 10 minutes, then allow to cool.

Stir in the egg yolk and sour cream. Season with salt and pepper.

Alternate layers of kohlrabi, radish, and apple into the greased baking dish. Cover with the sauce, bake for 7 minutes, then place under the broiler until golden brown.

Serve warm.

. . . .

Tip: Whisk the egg yolk into the cool kohlrabi liquid to prevent it from scrambling.

. . . .

Savory Apple Couscous

This dish makes a great accompaniment to pork or game. It is

also great on its own. Top it off with a scoop of vanilla ice cream,

and suddenly you have dessert.

1/4 cup dark rum
1/2 cup golden sultana raisins
2 cups couscous
2 tbsp. unsalted butter
2 baking apples, peeled, cored, diced
1/4 cup almonds, toasted, then crushed
1/4 tsp. cinnamon
1/4 tsp. allspice
1/8 cup maple syrup
1/4 cup instant rolled oats
1/4 cup finely diced aged cheddar cheese
1/8 cup flat leaf parsley, sliced

Heat the rum in a small bowl in the microwave then add the raisins, or heat on stove and pour over raisins in a small bowl. Cover bowl and set aside to soak.

Place couscous in a bowl, pour in 2 cups of boiling water, cover, and let sit for 5 to 10 minutes. Fluff with a fork.

In a large nonstick frying pan, melt the butter over medium heat. Sauté the apples and almonds for 5 minutes. Add spices, syrup, and oats, and sauté for 5 additional minutes, or until golden brown. Add the cheese and heat until cheese melts.

Add rum raisins and couscus to frying pan. Garnish with parsley and serve.

• •

Tip: Toasting nuts in the oven or in a pan before adding them to any recipe will bring out their natural oils and make them all the more flavorful.

• •

Say No to Fast Food!

Say No to Fast Food!

Say no to takeout: these quickie meals are great for a lunch or dinner on the fly. All you need is a few ingredients, a bit of chopping, and a dash of organization. Having ingredients precut, portioned, and ready to go helps you get these dishes together in a quick, easy flow. You are what you eat, so take control of your health by choosing quality ingredients, and remember that takeout isn't the only answer to being in a rush. Some of these dishes have components that need to be made in advance, but the extra effort makes the finished meal worthwhile.

Faster-Cooking Foods

Faster-Cooking Foods

Veal and Mushrooms

This one is an old classic. The combination of veal, mushrooms,

and wine is a real winner, and is a favorite amongst the ladies

in my family.

1/4 cup oil
1 lb. veal fillet or loin, thinly sliced
6 cups mushrooms (oyster, shiitake, cremini), sliced
1 small onion, minced
1 cup white wine
1 cup brown beef stock
1/2 cup whipping cream
1/2 tsp. Dijon mustard
1 tsp. lemon juice
1/4 cup sour cream
1/2 cup whipping cream, whipped
1/4 cup sliced chives

In a large pan over high heat, heat half the oil and sear both sides of the veal for about 3 minutes or until brown. Remove veal from the pan and keep warm.

In the same pan, sauté the mushrooms for about 4 minutes. Remove mushrooms from the pan and keep warm with the veal.

Add the remaining oil to the pan and sauté the onion until translucent. Reduce heat to medium high, add the wine, and reduce by 80%.

Add the beef stock and cream and reduce again by 50%. Remove the pan from the heat and add the meat juices from the warming plate. Add mustard, lemon juice, and sour cream, then whisk well.

Fold in the veal, mushrooms, and whipped cream. Garnish with chives.

. . . .

Tip: Use a hot pan, and sear the meat well. Don't shake the pan—shaking will cause the moisture to come out of the meat, and the meat will boil instead of braise.

. . . .

Vietnamese Caramelized Chicken

This recipe is inspired by my recollection of the signature dish at

a Vietnamese restaurant in San Francisco.

3/4 cup brown sugar
3 cups cold water
1/2 cup fish sauce
1/3 cup rice wine vinegar
1 tsp. soy sauce
1 tsp. ginger purée
4 cloves garlic, minced
1 drop sesame seed oil
1/4 cup vegetable oil
1 1/2 lbs. chicken thighs, boneless, skinless
5 scallions, finely sliced
2 jalapeño peppers, finely sliced
1 cup chopped roasted peanuts
1/2 cup bean sprouts
1/2 cup coriander sprigs

In a medium bowl, combine the brown sugar, cold water, fish sauce, rice wine vinegar, soy sauce, ginger, garlic, and sesame seed oil. Set aside.

In a large nonstick frying pan, heat half the oil on medium high and sear the chicken pieces until golden brown.

Add 1/3 of the brown-sugar sauce and stir until chicken is caramelized and the liquid has reduced completely.

Add remaining sauce and simmer until the chicken is tender and the sauce is syrupy.

Add the scallions and jalapeño peppers.

Garnish with peanuts, sprouts, and coriander sprigs, and serve with steamed rice or rice noodles.

. . . .

Tip: Searing the chicken really well and reducing the sauce in stages is what allows the chicken to caramelize into a deep, rich color. This is an absolutely easy dish to reheat—make it the day ahead!

. . . .

Spicy Peanut Chicken

A real hit at my West 50 Pourhouse and Grille. My rendition of chicken satay ditches the skewers and bumps the dish from appetizer to main course.

1 tsp. ground coriander
1 1/2 tbsp. lime juice, or the juice from 1 lime
1 small chili, seeds removed and sliced
1 1/2 lbs. chicken thighs, boneless
1/2 cup vegetable oil
1 cup salted peanuts
3 cloves garlic
1 tbsp. grated fresh ginger root
1 bunch scallions, whites only, sliced
4 cups chicken stock
1 tsp. Thai chili sauce
4 cups coconut milk
1 cup whipping cream
1/2 cup peanut butter
4 scallions, white only, chopped
1 bunch coriander, sliced

In a large bowl, combine the ground coriander, lime juice, and chilies. Add the chicken pieces and marinate for one hour.

In a large frying pan, heat half the oil over medium-high heat and sear the chicken pieces until golden brown on all sides. Remove from the pan and set aside.

To the same pan, add the rest of the oil, the peanuts, garlic, ginger, and sliced scallions and sauté for 3 to 4 minutes.

Add the chicken stock, bring to a boil, then turn heat down and simmer for 5 minutes.

Reduce the heat to medium-low, add the chili sauce, coconut milk, and cream, then whisk in the peanut butter. Add the chicken pieces and continue to simmer for 10 minutes. Taste and adjust seasonings if necessary.

Toss in the chopped scallions and coriander just before serving.

. . . .

Tip: I prefer to use chicken thighs for this recipe because the dark meat tends to stay moister. You can use breast meat if you like, but you will need to lessen the cooking time. The peanuts and peanut butter have a high salt content, so taste before seasoning.

. . . .

Bourbon Chicken and Shrimp Risotto

This dish brings together all the heart and soul of New Orleans cooking. It is a favorite at my restaurant On the Curve Hot Stove and Wine Bar. No need to rush if you want to try it there: I won't be taking it off the menu any time soon.

To make the risotto, see the Basic Risotto recipe on page 195.

Bourbon Chicken and Shrimp

1/4 cup vegetable oil
2 oz. andouille sausage, sliced
4 oz. chicken thighs, boneless, skinless, cut into strips
1 tbsp. unsalted butter
1 medium onion, sliced
2 tbsp. Cajun powder
1 tomato, coarsely chopped
1/2 sweet bell pepper, cubed
2 oz. bourbon
12 large shrimp, cleaned
3/4 cup tomato juice
1 cup sliced scallions, for garnish

Make the Basic Risotto (page 195); keep warm.

Place oil and sliced sausage in a large pan over medium-high heat; brown the sausage until crispy.

Add the chicken strips and brown until chicken is completely cooked.

Add butter and sliced onion. Sauté until onion is light brown.

Dust with Cajun powder and sauté for a few more minutes.

Add the tomato and pepper, then deglaze with the bourbon.

Add the shrimp and sauté until they turn orange and are completely cooked.

Fold in the warm risotto and the tomato juice. Adjust the seasoning to taste, and garnish with scallion slices.

. . . .

Tip: Toast the Cajun spices in a pan before you add them to the chicken; toasting gives the flavors extra bang.

. . . .

Mushroom and Spinach Strudel

Yet another classic! This is a great meatless alternative.

Mushroom and Spinach Strudel

2 cups button mushrooms
2 cups oyster mushrooms
2 cups cremini mushrooms
2 cups shiitake mushrooms
4 cups spinach
1 cup olive oil
1 small onion, chopped
1 clove garlic, minced
1/2 cup parsley, sliced
1/2 cup oregano, chopped
1 tbsp. lemon juice, or juice from half a lemon
1 tsp. lemon zest, or zest from half a lemon
4 oz. aged white cheddar cheese, grated
4 oz. goat's cheese, crumbled
salt and pepper to taste
Strudel Dough (page 197)
1/4 cup unsalted butter, melted
1 cup white bread crumbs
1 large egg
1/2 cup whole milk

Preheat the oven to 350°F.

Prepare the mushrooms by carefully cleaning then slicing into 1/4-inch pieces. Wash the spinach in cold running water to remove any grit or sand that clings to the leaves. Pat dry with paper towels.

In a large frying pan over high heat, heat the oil. Add mushrooms and onion and sauté until onion is golden brown.

Add the garlic and sauté until translucent. Stir in the spinach and herbs and remove from heat. Let the mixture cool, then fold in lemon juice, zest, cheeses, and bread crumbs. Season with salt and pepper.

Roll the pastry out to a rectangle 12" x 24" and 1/8" thick. Brush with melted butter and spread with the mushroom mixture leaving about 1/2 inch of pastry around the edges for sealing. Roll forward tightly and place on a baking sheet lined with parchment paper. Whisk together egg and milk, then brush onto rolled pastry. Bake for 20 minutes, or until pastry is golden brown.

Let cool to room temperature before cutting. Serve with Aioli Dip.

Aioli Dip

1 small gold-flesh potato
2 egg yolks, beaten
3 cloves garlic, minced
2 tbsp. lemon juice, or the juice from 1 lemon
salt and pepper to taste
2 cups olive oil

Cook the potato in salted water until tender. Peel and grate.

In a medium bowl, combine grated potato, egg yolks, garlic, lemon juice, salt, and pepper.

Quickly whisk in the olive oil and mix until blended.

. . . .

Tip: Use high heat and a pan with a large surface to cook mushrooms. Don't overfill the pan and don't flip the mushrooms around. Sear them until they are golden brown on all sides.

. . . .

Bratwurst-Stuffed Pork Tenderloin

Pork and carrots always make a great combination. Mustard and caraway make this sauce a true culinary delight, the Swiss chard is a palette cleanser, and the carrot juice gives the whole dish a zingy boost of flavor.

Bratwurst-Stuffed Pork Tenderloin

1 lb. (4 x 4-oz. portions) pork tenderloin
12 oz. bratwurst
2 tbsp. green peppercorns
2 tbsp. parsley, sliced
1 tsp. caraway seeds
1 head Swiss chard, washed, stems removed
4 strips bacon
1 small onion, diced
1/2 cup oil
1 large carrot, diced
1 tsp. honey
1 1/4 cups chicken stock
1 tsp. mustard
1/4 cup cream
1/4 tsp. cayenne pepper
salt
2 carrots, juiced

The aim here is to cut the tenderloin into a flat fillet. Cut into the tenderloin lengthwise about halfway, then continue to cut while simultaneously spreading the meat out from the center. Lay resulting rectangle of tenderloin on a sheet of parchment paper.

Remove the casings from the bratwurst and place the sausage mixture in a medium bowl. Mix in the green peppercorns, parsley, and caraway seeds.

Fill a medium bowl with cold water and a handful of ice. Set aside.

In a large pot, bring salted water to a boil. Blanch the Swiss chard for 1 minute then, using strainer or tongs, pull out the chard and cool in the ice bath to stop the cooking process. When completely cool, remove from the water and pat dry with a towel or paper towels.

Cover entire rectangle of tenderloin with bratwurst mixture, then add a layer of Swiss chard. Roll up the tenderloin and wrap with the bacon strips. Wrap the entire roll in tin foil and, time permitting, chill for at least one hour.

Preheat oven to 350°F.

Remove the foil and place the chilled tenderloin on a rack in a baking pan. Bake for about 18 minutes, or until the internal temperature is 145°F.

Place the tenderloin on a warmed plate and tent with tin foil. Allow to rest for at least 10 minutes.

Meanwhile, in a small pot, over medium heat, sauté the onion in the oil until onion is translucent. Add the carrots and honey. Cook for a few more minutes.

Add chicken stock and simmer until the carrots are tender.

Pour contents of pot into a blender or food processor. Add mustard, cream cayenne pepper, and salt. Blend until smooth. Be careful: this mixture is hot!

Return blended liquid to the pot and bring back up to heat. Just before serving, strain through a fine sieve and add the carrot juice. Place the tenderloin onto the plate and pour the liquid around the meat.

• •

Tip: Letting meat rest allows all the juices to settle, so they don't run out and get wasted when you slice the meat. The larger the piece of meat, the longer it should rest.

• •

South Beach Sandwiches

My son Nicolas and I had a run-in with authentic Cuban food while vacationing in Florida. The result is that we are now both addicted to these sandwiches. Turn them into an on-the-fly meal by making the pulled pork ahead of time—that way all you have to do is assemble the sandwiches.

2 onions, sliced
1 lb. pork loin roast
2 cups Olaf's Black Spice Rub (page 189)
2 cups chicken stock
4 oz. rum
1 baguette
 hot mustard
8 slices Swiss cheese
8 slices cooked ham
2 dill pickles, sliced

Preheat the oven to 350°F.

Place the sliced onions in a large roasting pan. Divide the pork roast into four portions and place on top of the onions.. Cover the roast portions with Olaf's Black Spice Rub. Pour in the chicken stock and rum. Cover and bake for one hour or until the internal temperature of the pork is 165°F. Remove from oven.

When the pork is cool enough to handle, but still warm, remove it from the pan and slice thinly, or shred it by pulling the meat apart with your fingers.

Place the roasting pan over medium heat and cook down the juices until most of the liquid has been absorbed by the onions. Add to the pork.

Slice open the baguette and spread both sides with mustard. Add a layer of Swiss cheese, a layer of ham, a layer of pork, another layer of cheese, and finally add the pickle slices. Close the baguette and cut into sections; place the sandwich sections on a baking tray and warm them in the oven for 3 minutes.

· ·

Tip: For maximum flavor, make sure you pour all the goodness from the roasting pan into the pork.

· ·

Olaf's Wiener Schnitzel

Inspired by my mom and my Oma, this is a signature dish in all of my restaurants. Serve with Lemon Caper Relish (recipe follows).

8 pork tenderloin scaloppini, 3 oz. each
salt and pepper
2 cups flour
2 cups milk
2 eggs
2 cups whipping cream, whipped
3 to 4 cups fresh bread crumbs
1/4 cup unsalted butter
vegetable oil for frying

Season the pork with salt and pepper. Pour flour into a flat dish. In a second dish, whisk the milk with the eggs and fold in the whipped cream. Put the bread crumbs in a third dish. Dredge each piece of pork in the flour, tap off any excess flour, then dip pork into the cream mixture. Finally, coat both sides with the bread crumbs. Chill for 30 minutes.

In a deep frying pan, heat the butter and oil on medium high and pan-fry the cutlets until golden brown. Transfer onto a paper towel and pat off any excess cooking oil.

Lemon Caper Relish

1/2 cup lemon juice, or the juice from 3 lemons
1 tsp. Dijon mustard
1/4 tsp. white pepper
2 cups olive oil
3 lemons, peeled, seeded, segmented
1/4 cup capers, drained
1 shallot, finely diced
1 tbsp. chervil, picked from the stalk
2 cups flat-leaf parsley, sliced
salt to taste

In a small bowl, combine the lemon juice, mustard, and pepper then slowly whisk in the olive oil until the mixture is lightly emulsified and coats the back of a spoon. Fold in the rest of the ingredients.

. . . .

Tip: Combining whipped cream with milk makes a much crispier coating. You could use veal or chicken instead of the pork.

. . . .

When you remove the lemon peel, be sure to remove the bitter pith; it's the fine white layer between the rind and the flesh.

Handmade and Delicate

German cuisine isn't known for its delicacy, let alone its noodles or pasta dishes, but I am going to change that. I have started by reducing portion sizes and refining hearty starches into soft and delicate morsels. These noodles can easily stand on their own, and I have treated them to some great sauces so that they can soak up big flavors that will make them a huge hit at any table. Once you get a handle on the noodle recipes, you can get personal and add some of your own sauce ideas. Treat these old-fashioned starchy sides as the new pastas of your kitchen.

Pasta, Noodles, and Dumplings

Focaccia Dumplings in Oyster Mushroom Sauce

Focaccia Dumplings

1 lb. focaccia bread, day old, cubed
1/2 cup olive oil
2 cloves garlic, sliced
2 cups spinach, washed
1 1/2 cups vegetable or chicken stock
3 eggs, beaten
1 cup sun-dried tomatoes, chopped
3/4 cup Parmesan cheese
1 cup basil, sliced
1 cup parsley, sliced
1 cup bread crumbs
4 oz. smoked mozzarella cheese, cubed
1 cup ricotta cheese
salt and pepper to taste
smoked paprika

In a large bowl, place the focaccia cubes and set aside.

In a large frying pan over medium heat, heat the olive oil and lightly brown the garlic slices then wilt the spinach leaves. Remove garlic and spinach from the pan. Set the pan aside, keeping the flavored oil; we will get back to it.

Add the garlic and spinach to the focaccia cubes and toss together.

In a medium pan over medium heat, warm the stock, then stir into the focaccia cubes. Mix well. While still warm, add the beaten eggs and quickly stir to combine well.

Add the tomatoes, Parmesan cheese, half the basil, and half the parsley. Form into golf ball–size dumplings. If mixture is too wet, add in some bread crumbs. With you finger, press a hole into the center of each dumpling and fill with a mozzarella cube, then press dumpling together to close the indent. Place filled dumplings on a tray and refrigerate for about 45 minutes.

Bring a large pot of salted water to a boil, carefully drop in the dumplings, cover, and simmer for 20 minutes, or until the dumplings float to the surface. Using a slotted spoon, remove dumplings.

In the frying pan you set aside, on medium heat, slightly crisp up the dumplings.

Before plating, roll the dumplings in the rest of the chopped basil and parsley.

In a small bowl, combine the ricotta cheese, salt, and pepper then spoon onto dumplings as a topping.

Dust with smoked paprika for presentation.

Oyster Mushroom Sauce

1/4 cup olive oil
3 cups oyster mushrooms, sliced
1 small white onion, diced
1 cup white wine
1 1/2 cups whipping cream
salt and pepper to taste
1/4 cup chives, sliced

In a small pan, add the olive oil and sauté the mushrooms. Transfer half of the mushrooms onto a small plate and set aside. Add the onion to the pan with the remaining mushrooms and sweat until the onions are translucent. Deglaze with the white wine and reduce by 80%. Add the cream and simmer for 5 minutes or until cream thickens enough to coat the back of a spoon. Season with salt and pepper. Purée the mixture in a blender or food processor then return to the pan. Add the reserved mushrooms; stir in chives. Serve immediately or simmer on very low until ready to serve.

Tip: Be patient when poaching the dumplings. It may seem like they're never going to float, but they will. This is generally the case for any dumpling or gnocchi.

Focaccia Dumplings in Oyster Mushroom Sauce

Potato Dumplings and Lobster in Sherry Tarragon Sauce

Potato Dumplings and Lobster in Sherry Tarragon Sauce

This is my German twist on the Italian gnocchi dumpling.

Potato Dumplings

1 1/2 lbs. yellow-flesh potato, skin on
1/2 cup flour
2 eggs
2 egg yolks
1/2 tsp. salt
1 tsp. white pepper
1/2 tsp. nutmeg
1/2 cup potato starch
1/2 cup extra flour for dredging

In a medium pot of salted water, cook the potatoes, skin on, until tender when poked with a fork. Drain very well. While still warm, peel the potatoes and press through a ricer. Place riced potato in a bowl and quickly fold in the flour, eggs, egg yolks, salt, pepper, nutmeg, and potato starch.

Portion the dumplings using a mini ice cream scoop or a tablespoon. Roll them into balls between the palms of your hands, then roll them in flour. Set on a tray lined with parchment paper then refrigerate for 30 minutes.

In a very large pot of boiling salted water, drop the dumplings and let simmer for 15 minutes or until they float to the surface. Place on paper towels to dry.

Lobster in Sherry Tarragon Sauce

1/2 cup olive oil
4 medium vine-ripened tomatoes, coarsely chopped
salt and pepper
1 tbsp. sugar
1/2 cup basil, sliced
1/2 cup oregano, sliced
3 tbsp. orange juice, or the juice from 1 orange
2 tsp. orange zest, or the zest from 1 orange
12 oz. lobster meat
4 oz. sherry
1 cup whipping cream
1/4 cup tarragon, leaves only, sliced
1/4 cup chives, sliced

Preheat the oven to 250°F.

In a large bowl, combine 1/4 cup of the oil, tomatoes, salt, pepper, sugar, basil, oregano, orange juice, and orange zest. Transfer to a baking sheet and roast for 30 minutes.

In a large frying pan over medium heat, heat remaining oil. Add lobster meat and roasted tomato mixture and sauté for 3 minutes.

Deglaze the pan with the sherry.

Add cream, then add the dumplings and slowly bring the liquids to a simmer.

Just before serving, add the tarragon and chives.

. . . .

Tip: When making any potato mixture, you must work with warm potatoes, and your mixing must go very quickly; otherwise any remaining water in the potatoes will make the mixture gluey.

. . . .

If you don't have a ricer, use a potato masher, but make sure the mixture is very well mashed and free of lumps.

Curried Shellfish with Red Beet Spaetzle

Curried Shellfish with Red Beet Spaetzle

Yet another inspiration from my experience in an Italian fine-dining restaurant. It was originally a red beet linguini but I put my own twist on it. You'll need to make Red Beet Spaetzle on page 194.

Curry Sauce

1/4 cup olive oil
1 small onion, diced
1 clove garlic, minced
1/4 tsp. fresh ginger root, minced
1/2 stalk lemongrass, chopped
2 1/2 tbsp. curry powder
1/4 tsp. cayenne pepper
2 cups coconut milk
1 cup whipping cream
salt and pepper

In a medium pot over medium-high heat, heat the oil. Add onion, garlic, ginger, and lemongrass and sauté for 5 minutes.

Reduce the temperature to medium. Dust with curry powder and cayenne pepper and sauté for a few minutes.

Deglaze with the coconut milk and cream, then simmer for 5 minutes.

Season to taste, then strain through a fine sieve into a small pot. Set aside.

Shellfish

1/4 cup olive oil
8 scallops
8 shrimp, cleaned
1 lb. mussels, washed and debearded
1 1/2 cups white wine
salt and pepper
1 recipe Red Beet Spaetzle (page 194)
1 head broccoli florets, blanched
1 pint pea and broccoli sprouts

In a large pan over high heat, heat the oil and sear the scallops for 1 minute on each side to caramelize. Remove from pan and set aside.

Caramelize shrimp and remove from pan.

Add the mussels, white wine, salt, and pepper to the pan and cover for 5 minutes until most of the mussels have opened. Discard any unopened mussels.

Return the scallops and shrimp to the pan. Add the curry sauce. Warm the spaetzle in a pot of boiling water, strain, and add to the sauce. Toss in the broccoli.

Garnish with sprouts and serve immediately.

· ·

Tip: Sear the shellfish then set aside. They will continue to cook as they wait to be added to the warm sauce.

· ·

Spaetzle and Clams in White Wine

My version of Germany meeting Italy. You'll need to make the

noodles beforehand: you'll find the recipe for Basic Spaetzle on

page 192.

1/2 cup olive oil
4 cloves garlic, sliced
2 lbs. Littleneck clams
salt and pepper
2 bay leaves
1 small white onion, minced
3 cups dry white wine
1 lemon, juice and zest
3/4 cup ice-cold unsalted butter, cut into cubes
1 cup parsley, sliced
4 cups Spaetzle noodles (page 192)
1/2 cup olive oil

In a large soup pot, over medium-high heat, heat the olive oil and sauté the garlic until brown. Add the clams. Stir in salt and pepper, bay leaves, onion, and wine. Cover the pot with a tight-fitting lid, shake, and simmer for approximately 7 minutes or until all or most of the clams are open. Discard bay leaves and any unopened clams. Remove all the opened clams and take the flesh out of the shells.

Return the pot of liquid to the stove over medium heat and add the lemon juice and zest. Quickly whisk in the butter cubes until the sauce thickens and becomes glossy. Add the clams back into the sauce. Taste and adjust the seasoning if necessary.

Toss in the parsley and noodles. Serve on warm plates and drizzle with olive oil.

. . . .

Tip: Make sure you don't reduce the liquid too much. The clam juice is the heart and soul of this dish.

. . . .

Whole Wheat Spaetzle
with Mushrooms

This meatless dish is a true down-to-earth recipe. It has so many

great flavors that you just want to double the recipe and eat it for

days. You'll need to make Whole Wheat Spaetzle, which can be

found on page 193.

1/3 cup olive oil
4 cloves garlic, sliced
4 cups mixed mushrooms (cremini, shiitake, oyster)
1/2 cup basil, sliced
1 cup parsley, sliced
1/2 cup oregano, chopped
1 tsp lemon zest, or the zest from half a fresh lemon
2 cups chicken stock
1/4 cup unsalted butter, ice-cold, cut into cubes
Whole Wheat Spaetzle (page 193)
2 tbsp. lemon, juice, or the juice from 1 fresh lemon
sea salt
cracked pepper
1 cup Parmigiano Reggiano cheese, grated
1 bunch arugula, sliced

In a large pot over medium heat, heat the oil and sauté the garlic slices until light brown. Add the mushrooms and cook until golden brown.

Add the herbs and lemon zest. Deglaze with chicken stock. Add the butter cubes and stir quickly until sauce thickens and becomes glossy.

Toss in the prepared noodles, season with lemon juice, salt, and pepper, then add cheese and arugula.

. . . .

Tip: The broth must be hot and simmering when you add the ice-cold butter.

. . . .

Beef Tenderloin with Blue Cheese Spaetzle and Port Wine Reduction

Beef Tenderloin with Blue Cheese Spaetzle and Port Wine Reduction

This is a creation that my friend Simon Cox and I came up with. I call the combination of beef, port, and blue cheese the Three Deadly Sins of Eating. You'll need to prepare the noodles and port wine ahead of time. Make the Basic Spaetzle recipe on page 192 and Port Wine Reduction recipe on page 186.

1 lb. beef tenderloin
salt and pepper
1/4 cup plus 1 tbsp. olive oil
1 small white onion, finely diced
1 cup white wine
3/4 cup whipping cream
salt and white pepper to taste
3/4 cup blue cheese
1/4 cup Parmesan cheese, grated
4 cups Basic Spaetzle noodles (page 192)
1/4 cup parsley, sliced
2 tsp. cracked coarse pepper
2 scallions, sliced
1 recipe Port Wine Reduction (page 186)
1 cup blue cheese, crumbled

Preheat the oven to 350°F.

Season the tenderloin with salt and pepper. In a large frying pan that can be trasferred to the oven, over high heat, heat 1 tbsp. olive oil. Sear the tenderloin on all sides. Place the pan in the oven and bake the tenderloin for approximately 7 minutes, or until the internal temperature of the meat is 130°F. Cover with a loose foil tent and let rest for at least 10 minutes. Thinly slice against the grain. Set aside.

Heat 1/4 cup oil in a small pot on medium heat and sauté the onion until translucent. Deglaze with the white wine and reduce by 80%. Add the cream. Simmer for 3 minutes.

Season and strain through a fine mesh sieve into a clean saucepan. Bring to a simmer and fold in the cheeses. Season with salt and pepper, then add noodles, parsley, cracked pepper, and scallions, and toss together.

Serve on a large platter, or divide onto individual serving plates. Place the beef slices on the side. Spoon the Port Reduction over the top of the tenderloin and garnish with crumbled blue cheese.

Crab and Smoked Salmon Ravioli with Maple Glaze

You'll need to make the Basic Ravioli on page 196.

Filling

1 tbsp. unsalted butter
1 small onion, finely diced
1/2 cup smoked salmon, sliced
3/4 cup crabmeat
1 tbsp. dill, chopped
1 tbsp. chives, sliced
1/2 tsp. Dijon mustard
1 tsp. lemon zest, or the zest from half a fresh lemon
1/2 cup sour cream

In a medium frying pan over medium heat, melt the butter, then sauté onion until light brown. Add smoked salmon, then transfer to a large bowl.

Add remaining ingredients and chill.

Make the ravioli dough by following the Basic Ravioli recipe on page 196, then follow the directions for your pasta machine to roll out the dough gradually from thick to thin. If using a rolling pin, it will take a while to work the dough down to about 1/16-inch in thickness.

Cut the ravioli dough into 4-inch squares. You will need 8 squares in total. Make a mound of about 2 tbsp. of the stuffing mixture in the center of the ravioli squares. Make an egg wash with the egg and milk and cover the perimeter of the squares. Cover with another sheet of ravioli dough and seal firmly with a scalloped pastry roller or your fingers. When ready to serve, blanch the ravioli in boiling salted water for 3 minutes until tender.

. . . .

Tip: If you are concerned about making your own ravioli dough, a good quality store-bought dough would also work.

. . . .

Maple Glaze

1 tbsp. butter
2 slices smoked salmon
3/4 cup maple syrup
salt and pepper to taste
1/4 cup dill, chopped
1 cup corn niblets (canned is fine)

In a large frying pan over medium heat, melt the butter, then heat until brown and foaming.

Add the smoked salmon and continue browning. Add the maple syrup and reduce liquid by 50%, or until salmon looks like marmalade.

Add the salt, pepper, dill, and corn niblets.

Place on serving plates. Drizzle the Maple Glaze onto ravioli just before serving.

Veal Ravioli

This is how a German chef tries to be Italian. Let me know how

I'm doing. You'll need to prepare the Basic Ravioli on page 196.

Filling

1/4 cup vegetable oil
1 small onion, finely diced
1 clove garlic, minced
1/4 lb. ground veal
1 cup frozen spinach, thawed, drained, chopped
2 cups pecorino cheese, grated
1/2 cup fresh white bread crumbs
1/4 cup milk
2 tbsp. parsley, sliced
salt and black pepper to taste
1 recipe Basic Ravioli (page 196)

In a large pan, heat oil over medium heat. Sauté the onion, garlic, and veal until the veal is cooked through. Drain off any excess oil. Add the remaining ingredients. The mixture should be dry but tacky to the touch. Chill in the refrigerator while you make the ravioli dough.

Fill ravioli with the chilled veal mixture then cook in a large pot of boiling salted water until the ravioli float to the surface. Remove with a slotted spoon.

Sauce

1/2 cup olive oil
3 cloves garlic, minced
2 tbsp. pine nuts
1 tbsp. sage, sliced
1 small onion, finely diced
1 bulb fennel, diced
2 tsp. lemon zest, or the zest of 1 large lemon
3 tbsp. lemon juice, or juice from 1 large lemon
2 cups chicken stock
1 cup dried black olives, available at grocery stores
salt and pepper to taste
1/2 cup parsley, sliced
1 tbsp. olive oil

In a medium pot over medium-high heat, heat the oil. Add the garlic and pine nuts and sauté. Add the sage, onion, fennel, lemon zest, and lemon juice and sauté for a few minutes.

Add the chicken stock, olives, salt, and pepper and bring to a slow boil.

Add the warm ravioli; add parsley.

Drizzle with olive oil and serve.

. . . .

Tip: The secret of soft veal filling or meatballs is that the bread crumbs and milk combine to form a paste.

. . . .

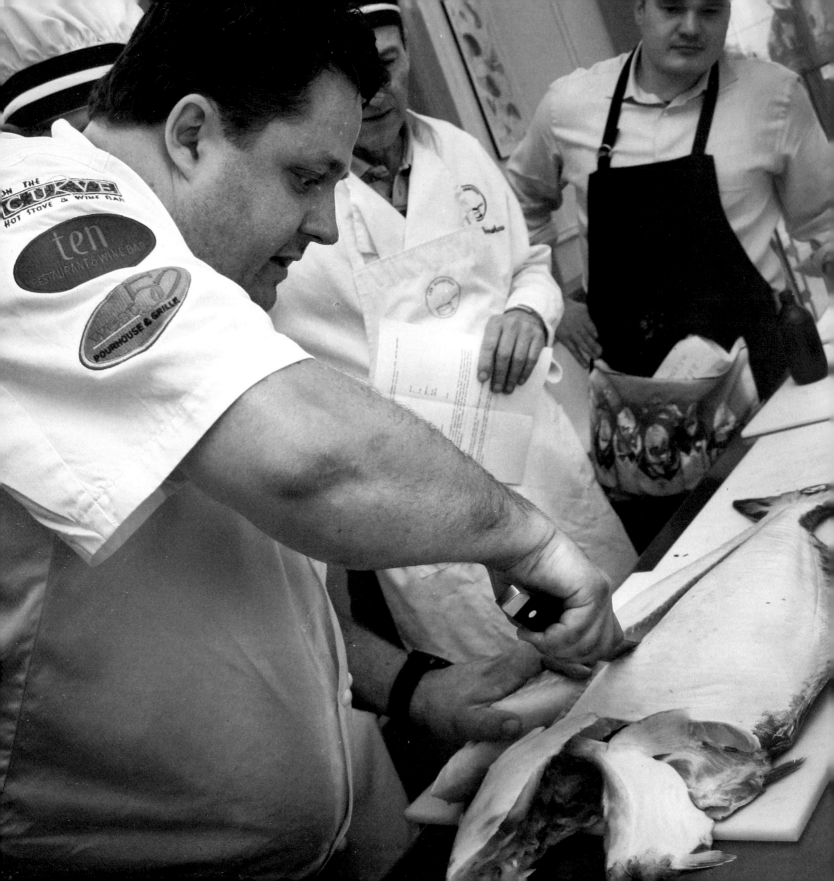

Fresh and Light

My Opa passed his passion for fish on to me when I was a boy. He was on his second visit to Canada and wanted to experience Canadian fishing firsthand. We thought it a little odd that he demanded two fishing rods but happily fulfilled his request. It turns out he was on to something. The next few hours were spent with my Opa pulling one fish after another off both his fishing lines. The sight of him zipping from rod to rod was a riot. I can still see the whole thing as if I was right there. His catch was the biggest I have ever seen in my whole life.

Fast-forward several years to me honing my craft in a posh Berlin hotel and, yet again, my Opa's zeal for fish was contagious. The Spree River feeds Berlin with some of the world's best freshwater fish. Its banks are lined with little markets and smoke huts. So, anytime we had the chance to get together on Fridays, my Opa and I would head out to the markets or a restaurant and have a fabulous lunch together.

I cannot say enough good things about fish. As far as I'm concerned every day can be fish Friday. No matter how you prepare your fish, always be mindful of not overcooking it. Fish can be flaky but should never be cooked to the point of being dry and crumbly.

Fresh and Light

Fish

Seafood Soup

Never being able to find a great recipe for seafood soup or stew

prompted me to concoct this in one of my own kitchens. Now it

is one of the signature soups of my menus.

1/2 cup olive oil
4 cloves garlic, sliced
1 small onion, diced
1 tbsp. basil, sliced
1 tbsp. oregano, sliced
1 tbsp. thyme, chopped
1 lb. mussels
1 lb. Littleneck clams
1 red chili pepper, sliced
1 tbsp. smoked paprika
4 vine-ripened tomatoes, diced
2 roasted red peppers, sliced
1 tsp. saffron
3 cups white wine
3 cups vegetable stock
2 squid, sliced into rings
1 chorizo, quartered
1/2 lb. cod, diced
4 mini white potatoes, steamed and peeled
12 pearl onions, steamed and peeled
8 cloves garlic, roasted
12 green olives

To a large pot over medium-high heat, add the olive oil, sliced garlic, and diced onion. Sauté until onion is golden brown.

Add basil, oregano, thyme, mussels, and clams. Cover and sauté for 5 minutes; the shellfish will open. Discard any un-opened mussels or clams.

With a slotted spoon, remove the mussels and clams and set aside. To the pot add chili pepper, paprika, tomatoes, one roasted pepper, and saffron. Sauté for 5 minutes then deglaze with white wine. Add vegetable stock and simmer for 15 minutes.

Pour contents of pot into a blender or food processor and purée, then strain through a fine sieve into a clean bowl. Set aside.

Pull the meat out of the cooled shellfish; set aside.

Add a splash of olive oil to two large pans. In one pan, sauté the squid and chorizo for about 3 minutes. Toss in the shellfish meat and heat through.

In the second pan, place the cod, potatoes, pearl onions, garlic, the remaining red pepper, and olives. Toss until warmed through.

Have hot soup bowls ready. Divide the sausage and shellfish amongst the bowls. Do the same with the vegetables. Pour in the hot soup purée.

. . . .

Tip: Serve this soup piping hot. Adjust the heat of the spices by modifying the amount of red chili peppers you use. When working with chili peppers, be very careful not to touch your face—the pepper oil on your fingers will burn your skin.

. . . .

Clams Casino Style

I ate my first clams in Atlantic City. I have made my way through

several big bowls of clams since then, and this is the recipe I like

best. It's a little bit of good and bad for you all rolled into one.

20 medium-sized Littleneck clams
1/2 cup olive oil
1 cup roasted red peppers, minced
1 cup green pepper, finely chopped
1 head garlic, roasted and minced
1/4 cup unsalted butter, melted
2 cups white bread crumbs
salt and pepper to taste
1/4 cup parsley, sliced
2 slices smoked bacon, cut into small cubes

Preheat the oven to 350°F.

Under cold running water, scrub the clamshells to remove all traces of sand and whiskers.

Carefully open the clams, remove the top shells, and loosen clams from bottom shells.

In a small bowl, combine the oil, peppers, garlic, butter, bread crumbs, salt, pepper, and parsley to make what I call "casino stuffing." Fill the half-shelled clams with the casino stuffing and top with bacon cubes.

Place clams on a baking pan and bake for 12 minutes. Remove from the oven; turn on the broiler. Place clams under the broiler for an additional 3 minutes to crisp up the bacon and filling.

. . . .

Tip: Please make sure the clams are the absolute freshest. When opening the clams, take your time and be careful using the knife.

. . . .

Salmon with Cucumber Spaghetti and Mustard Mousse

You'll need to prepare the Citrus Vinaigrette on page 206.

The Salmon

4 6-ounce center-cut wild salmon fillets, skin on
salt and pepper to taste
2 tbsp. olive oil

Preheat the oven to 400°F.

Cut half-inch slices into the skin of the salmon fillet.

Season the salmon on both sides. In a hot ovenproof pan with a little olive oil, sear the fish with the skin facing up for about 2 minutes, or until golden brown.

Turn the fillet skin-side down. Put the whole pan into the oven and bake for 10 minutes or until the internal temperature reaches 135°F.

Salmon with Cucumber Spaghetti and Mustard Mousse

Cucumber Spaghetti

1 cucumber
1/2 bunch dill, chopped
1 tbsp. dill seeds
3 tbsp. lemon juice, or the juice from 1 lemon
1 box sweet pea sprouts
1 recipe Citrus Vinaigrette (page 206)

Using a turning slicer, spin the cucumber into spaghetti strands. If you do not have a turning slicer, cut the cucumber into ribbons using a vegetable peeler.

In a medium bowl, gently toss the cucumber strands with the rest of the ingredients.

Mustard Mousse

1 tbsp. olive oil
1 small onion, finely diced
1 tbsp. tarragon, sliced
1/2 tsp. cracked peppercorns
3/4 cup dry white wine
3 gelatin sheets
3 egg yolks
3 tbsp. Dijon mustard
3 tbsp. lemon juice, or the juice of 1 lemon
2 tsp. lemon zest, or the zest of 1 lemon
salt and pepper
1 tbsp. grainy mustard
1 cup whipping cream, whipped

To a small pot over medium heat, add the olive oil and sauté the onion, lemon zest, tarragon, and peppercorns until the onion is translucent. Deglaze with white wine and reduce liquid by 75%. Strain through a fine sieve; set aside.

In a small bowl of cold water, soak the gelatin sheets to soften.

In a double boiler, or in a stainless-steel bowl over a pot of boiling water, whisk the egg yolks. Add the white wine mixture and whisk until thick ribbons form. Remove from the heat and add the Dijon mustard.

Add the gelatin sheets and continue to whisk until the gelatin is completely dissolved.

Add the lemon juice, salt, pepper, and grainy mustard. Cool to room temperature then fold in the whipped cream.

Pour into a bowl or individual dishes and refrigerate for about 1 hour to set.

Plate the cucumber spaghetti; perch the salmon on top and serve with the mustard mousse.

. . . .

Tip: Cutting slices into the salmon skin prevents the fish from buckling when you sear it.

. . . .

A turning slicer is a Japanese spinning mandolin that cuts fruits and vegetables into a never-ending shoestring—it's a must-have in my kitchen.

The individual dishes can be served beside the salmon. Or hand scoop the mousse on top of the fish right before serving.

Simple Salmon with Crudités Salad

This one is for real salmon lovers. I am talking perfect salmon fillets every time. Read this through, and you will be very surprised how I do it—it's a real conversation piece. You'll need to make a batch of the Citrus Vinaigrette on page 206.

Simple Salmon

4 7-oz. wild salmon fillets
4 plastic sealable bags
zest of 1 lemon
1 cup dill sprigs
1/4 cup maple syrup
sea salt
cracked pepper
1/4 cup sunflower seed oil

Place a salmon fillet in each sealable bag. Whisk the remaining ingredients and divide equally among the bags. Move the salmon fillets around in the bags to coat all sides.

In a large stockpot, bring about 20 cups of water to a boil. Turn off the heat and wait about 5 minutes, or until the water is 122°F. Add the salmon bags and let them float in the hot water until salmon is cooked, about 13 minutes. Remove and serve.

Crudités Salad

1 bulb fennel, finely sliced
1 medium carrot, finely sliced
5 green onions, finely sliced
8 red radishes, finely sliced
1 small red onion, finely sliced
1 small cucumber, finely sliced
2 pink grapefruits, peeled and broken into sections
1/2 cup chervil leaves, picked
1/2 cup chives, sliced
1 recipe Citrus Vinaigrette (page 206)

Place vegetables in an ice bath until you serve.

Drain the vegetable slices very well, add the herbs, then add Citrus Vinaigrette and grapefruits and toss.

To serve, place dressed salad in a shallow bowl, make a well in the center, and place the salmon on top.

· ·

Tip: Make sure you get enough of the oil in each bag so the fish will slide out of the bag easily after cooking.

· ·

Whiskey Maple Salmon with Potato Lox

I'm not sure if this dish is breakfast or dinner. The loaded lox potatoes and the maple salmon are a hit every night at my Ten Restaurant & Wine Bar.

Potato Lox

1 tbsp. unsalted butter
2 oz. smoked salmon
1/4 cup onion, finely diced
1/4 cup green onion, sliced
1/2 cup capers
5 medium potatoes, diced, steamed tender
1/2 cup cream cheese, room temperature
1 tbsp. dill, chopped
1/2 cup sour cream

In a medium pot over medium-high heat, heat the butter until foaming and light brown. Fry the smoked salmon until brown. Add the onions and capers, remove from heat, add the remaining ingredients, and keep warm.

Whiskey Maple Syrup

1/4 cup vegetable oil
1 small onion, finely diced
1/4 cup brown sugar
1/2 cup apple juice
2 oz. whiskey
1/2 cup maple syrup
1 tsp. fresh ginger root, minced

In a small pot over medium heat, heat the oil and sauté the onion until golden brown.

Add the brown sugar and caramelize. Add the remaining ingredients, reduce the heat, and reduce by 2/3 or until you have a syrup-like consistency.

Strain through a fine sieve; set aside.

The Salmon

4 cedar planks, store purchased
salt and pepper to taste
4 6-ounce Atlantic salmon, center-cut fillets, skin on
2 tbsp. vegetable oil

Preheat the oven to 400°F.

Toast and char the cedar planks in the oven for about 10 minutes.

Salt and pepper the salmon on both sides. In a hot pan with oil, sauté the fish with the skin facing up for about 2 minutes or until golden brown.

Place fillets skin side down near one end of the smooth side of cedar planks. Glaze with Whiskey Maple Syrup.

Place a portion of Potato Lox on the other end of the plank.

Bake for 10 minutes or until the internal temperature of the fish reaches 135°F.

Just before serving, broil for 2 to 3 minutes to give the dish a crispy finish.

· ·

Tip: Most wood planks have a smooth side and a coarse side. Use the smooth side for plating food.

· ·

Sole on Fridays

On the rare Friday lunch that I didn't work, my Opa and I would make our way to Berlin's *Kaufhaus des Westens*, informally known as the KaDeWe. It is truly one of the world's finest department stores. We loved the top floor, where every type of food and drink from around the world could be found. Spectacular food displays and mini eating stands were sprinkled throughout the entire floor. For food lovers, going up the escalator to the top floor was like taking a ride to heaven. We were not alone in our quest, however, and going on Fridays meant standing in line. You, on the other hand, get to skip the wait. Whole roasted baby sole coming up!

The Sole

4 6-ounce sole fillets, pin bones and skins removed
sea salt and pepper
1 tsp. smoked paprika
1/4 cup flour
1/2 cup olive oil
1 tsp. unsalted butter

Season sole fillets with salt and pepper. Combine smoked paprika and flour; dredge fillets in the mixture, then pat off excess flour.

In a large frying pan over medium-high heat, heat olive oil and butter. Sear fish for about 2 minutes on each side, or until golden brown.

Carefully transfer fish from pan to paper towel to remove excess oils.

Grainy Mustard Riesling

1/4 cup olive oil
1 small onion, diced
1 tbsp. golden sultana raisins
3 tbsp. lemon juice, or the juice from 1 lemon
2 tsp. lemon zest, or the zest from 1 lemon
1 bay leaf
1 tsp. capers
2 cups Riesling wine
1/3 cup whipping cream
1 tbsp. unsalted butter, ice-cold, cut into cubes
salt and pepper to taste
1 tsp. capers
1 tbsp. grainy mustard

In a small pot heat the olive oil and sauté the onion until translucent. Add raisins, lemon juice and zest, bay leaf, and 1 tsp. capers.

Continue to sauté for 3 minutes, then deglaze with the Riesling wine.

Reduce by 50%. Add in the cream and simmer for 5 minutes.

Whisk in cold butter, season, then strain mixture through a fine mesh strainer into a clean pot.

Bring to a simmer. Just before dressing plates, stir in remaining 1 tsp. capers and the grainy mustard.

· ·

Tip: Do not overcook fish. If the fish is very flaky and breaks into pieces on the way to the plate, then it's overcooked. Fish should be firm and solid.

· ·

Crab-Crusted Cedar-Planked Halibut

A big hit and signature dish at On the Curve! This dish cannot come off the menu—the customers would revolt.

Crab Crust

1/4 cup unsalted butter
1 leek, white only, finely sliced
1 cup chives, sliced
2 egg yolks
1 tbsp. Dijon mustard
2 cups (8 oz.) crabmeat
3 tbsp. lemon juice, or the juice from 1 lemon
2 tsp. lemon zest, or the zest from 1 lemon
salt and pepper to taste

In a small pot over medium heat, melt the butter then sauté the leek until wilted.

In a mixing bowl, combine the wilted leeks and the remaining ingredients. Mix until just combined. Set aside.

The Halibut

4 cedar planks, store purchased
4 6-oz. halibut fillets, skinless
salt and pepper to taste
1 tbsp. olive oil
1 tsp. unsalted butter

Preheat the oven to 400°F.

Place cedar planks in the oven to toast and char—about 10 minutes.

Season the halibut with salt and pepper. In a large frying pan, heat the oil and sear fillets for about 2 minutes on each side.

Place the fillets on the hot planks and top with Crab Crust.

Bake for 10 minutes or until the internal temperature of the fillets reaches 145°F.

Lemon Garlic White Wine Butter Sauce

1 tbsp. butter
1 small onion, minced
2 cups white wine
1 bay leaf
1/4 cup whipping cream
2 cloves garlic, sliced
1/2 cup cold butter, cut into cubes
salt
1 tsp. cracked peppercorns
6 tbsp. lemon juice, or the juice from 2 lemons

In a small pot on medium heat, melt the butter and sauté onion and garlic. Add the white wine and bay leaf and reduce by at least 50%, or until no liquid remains.

Add the cream.

Remove pot from the heat and gradually add cold butter cubes, whisking constantly.

Strain the mixture through a fine sieve into a clean small dish, season to taste with salt and pepper, then add the lemon juice.

· ·

Tip: Halibut should be white, shiny, and firm. As well, the flesh should bounce back when pressed.

· ·

Crab-Crusted Cedar-Planked Halibut

Italian-Scented Cod with Potato Strings

If fish and chips came from Italy, this is how it would look!

Artichoke Purée

1 large yellow-flesh potato, peeled
1 1/2 cups canned artichokes, puréed
3 tbsp. lemon juice, or the juice from 1 lemon
1/4 cup olive oil
salt and pepper

Fill a small pot with water and bring to a boil, then cook potato over medium-high heat until fork tender. Drain well.

Using a hand blender, purée the potato until creamy.

Return potato to pot. Place over medium heat, then add the artichokes and lemon juice. Heat until just warmed up.

Slowly whisk in the olive oil.

Season with salt and pepper to taste; set aside.

Tomato and Red Pepper Relish

3 plum tomatoes, diced
2 red peppers, roasted and diced
1 cup sugar
1 stick cinnamon
1 bay leaf
1 cup sherry vinegar

In a medium pot over medium-high heat, combine all the ingredients and reduce liquid by 70% or until you have a relish-like consistency.

The Cod and Potato Strings

1/3 cup oregano leaves, ground
2 tsp. lemon zest, or the zest from 1 lemon
1 tbsp. sea salt
2 large yellow-flesh potatoes
4 4-ounce cod fillet, skinless, boneless
1 tbsp. olive oil
salt and pepper
4 cups vegetable oil for frying

Combine oregano, lemon zest, and sea salt in a small bowl; set aside.

Cut the potatoes on a turning slicer. (If you do not have a turning slicer, cut the potatoes into ribbons using a vegetable peeler.)

Toss the cod fillets in olive oil, then season with salt and pepper.

In a medium pot over medium-high heat, heat the vegetable oil to 275°F.

Hold the tops of the potato strings and carefully place them in the hot oil till they're submerged. Watch carefully, as they will brown quickly. Using a slotted spoon, transfer the strings to a baking tray lined with paper towels to absorb the excess oil.

Carefully let the fish slide into the hot oil and fry for approximately 4 minutes. Place on a baking sheet lined with paper towel to absorb any excess oil. Season immediately with oregano and lemon zest mixture.

To plate, place a large dollop of Artichoke Purée in the middle of the plate. Place the potatoes and fish on top and spoon the Tomato Red Pepper Relish on the side.

· ·

Tip: A turning slicer is a Japanese spinning mandolin that cuts fruits and vegetables into a never-ending shoestring.

· ·

Italian-Scented Cod with Potato Strings

Seared, Grilled, and Roasted

Seared, Grilled, and Roasted

Yes, I am a meat and potatoes boy. Most of my cooking years I have been part butcher and part *saucier* (the person in the kitchen who prepares all the restaurant's meats and sauces). Because of my years of practice, this chapter is second nature for me. To start off, you need to have a butcher you can trust. Not so easy considering all the super supermarkets out there these days, but they are around. The ideal is to find a local shop and stick with that. Chances are it will support local farmers by carrying local product. Your butcher can help you pick meats that are aged and cut according to your recipe needs. You may want to get out your white hat, because the dishes in this chapter run the gamut from casual cooking to full-on culinary challenge. Whether they are done in the oven or on a grill, all these recipes are meant to be fun.

Meat and Poultry

Meat and Poultry

Chicken and Veal Involtini

I came up with this creation when I catered an outdoor wedding for 350 guests. An Italian wedding where chicken and veal are served in just one slice.

White Wine Sauce

1/4 cup olive oil
1 white onion, diced
2 cups white wine
1 bay leaf
3 tbsp. lemon juice, or the juice from 1 lemon
2 tsp. lemon zest, or the zest from 1 lemon
1/3 cup whipping cream
1 cup chicken stock
salt and papper
1 tbsp. butter, cold, cut into cubes
1/4 cup capers
1 tbsp. parsley, sliced
1 lemon, cut into segments

In a small pot on medium heat, heat the olive oil and sauté the onion. Add the white wine, bay leaf, lemon juice, and zest and reduce by 90%, or until no liquid remains.

Add the cream and reduce by 90%; large bubbles should begin to appear. Add the chicken stock and heat to a simmer.

Strain the mixture through a fine sieve into a clean pot and check the seasoning. Before serving, whisk in the cold butter cubes then add the capers, parsley, and lemon segments.

Basil Marsala Cream Sauce

6 leaves basil, sliced
1/4 cup olive oil
1 small onion or shallot, finely diced
1 cup white wine
1/4 cup basil, sliced
1 bay leaf
1 cup whipping cream
1/2 cup Marsala wine
salt and white pepper to taste

Cut the 6 basil leaves into fine strips and set aside.

In a small pot on medium heat, add the olive oil and sauté the onion or shallot until translucent.

Deglaze with the white wine, then add 1/4 cup basil and the bay leaf. Reduce liquid by 80%, then add the cream and Marsala wine. Simmer for 5 minutes at medium temperature until liquid is reduced by 25%.

Season and strain through a sieve into a clean pot. Bring to a simmer, then stir in the finely sliced basil just before serving.

Veal Stuffing

1 1/4 lbs. veal sirloin
6 cups spinach
2 eggs
1/2 cup whipping cream
1/2 cup pine nuts, toasted
1 clove garlic, roasted
1 cup Gorgonzola cheese

Trim and square up the veal sirloin. Save the trimmings and set aside.

Cut the sirloin through the middle about 90% of the way. Open it up to make a large rectangle. Pound with a meat mallet until 1/4-inch thick. Place on plastic wrap and roll up. Place in the refrigerator until needed.

In a blender or food processor, blend the veal trimmings and spinach. Blend until smooth then add the eggs. Continue to blend while very slowly adding the cream. Scrape mixture into a bowl and add the toasted pine nuts, roasted garlic, and Gorgonzola cheese. Cover and refrigerate.

The Chicken

2 1/2 lb. whole chicken
6 oz. chicken breast meat
1/2 cup basil
2 eggs
salt and pepper
1/2 cup whipping cream
4 oz. smoked provolone cheese, cut into small cubes
4 oz. pancetta (Italian bacon), chopped
1/2 cup sun-dried tomatoes
1/2 cup toasted pistachio nuts

Debone the whole chicken, discard all the bones and cartilage, wrap the chicken in plastic wrap, and refrigerate.

In a blender or food processor, blend the chicken breast, basil, eggs, salt, and pepper until blended. Very slowly drizzle in the cream, then run the machine just until blended. Scrape the mixture into a bowl. Fold in the cheese cubes, pancetta, tomatoes, and pistachio nuts.

Assembly

Preheat the oven to 350°F

Roll out the veal sirloin and spread the veal mixture evenly across the length of the rectangle down one edge. Tightly roll up the sirloin. Wrap in plastic wrap, then in foil. Twist the ends of the foil to keep the roll tight; refrigerate.

Spread out a large piece of parchment paper and lay out the boneless chicken in the shape of a rectangle about 8 x 12 inches

(approx. size). Spread chicken stuffing mixture evenly across the boneless chicken. Unwrap the chilled veal roll and place in the middle of the chicken rectangle. Using the parchment paper as leverage, wrap the chicken around the veal roll, then pull the parchment paper around the new roll. Wrap the new roll in foil, then twist the ends to ensure the roll stays quite tight. Refrigerate for at least 1 hour to rest.

Remove wrapped roll from refrigerator and place on a rack in a roasting pan. Bake for approximately 1 hour, or until the internal temperature reaches 170°F. Let rest for about 20 minutes.

Remove paper and foil from the cooked roll and place back on the rack in the baking pan and place under the broiler for about 7 minutes to crisp up the roll.

Cut the rolled meats into 8 slices, plate, and add a tablespoon each of the White Wine and Basil Marsala Cream sauces.

Serves 8.

· ·

Tip: During the baking stage, don't let the oven get hotter than 350°F. If you do, the roll will definitely explode: the stuffing is highly sensitive to temperature.

· ·

Chicken and Veal Involtini

Stuffed Cornish Hen

This is a more advanced cook's recipe. It has a lot of diversity and when presented, it gives you and your guests a tremendous amount of satisfaction.

2 Cornish hens

Preheat oven to 400°F.

Debone Cornish hens and set the boneless intact hens aside and refrigerate.

Natural Hen Sauce

2 tbsp. olive oil
1/2 lb. chicken bones
2 large vine-ripened tomatoes, diced
1 onion, diced
1 stalk celery, diced
1 carrot, diced
4 cups chicken stock
1/2 cup thyme leaves

In an oven-proof roasting pan, heat oil. Add hen and chicken bones and sauté, then place in the oven and roast until brown.

After about 20 minutes through the browning stage, add diced tomatoes, onion, celery, and carrot, and continue to bake for 20 minutes.

Return roasting pan to stovetop and add chicken stock and thyme.

Using a fine slotted spoon, skim away any fat or grey foaming particles.

Reduce the liquid by 80% and pass through a fine sieve into a clean pot.

Check the seasoning and reduce further until the sauce coats the back of the spoon.

Filling

salt and pepper
1 tbsp. toasted green pistachios
1/4 red pepper, very finely diced
1 tbsp. European double-smoked bacon, finely diced
2 chicken breasts
1/2 tsp. English mustard powder
3/4 cup whipping cream
2 egg whites
4 strips bacon
2 sprigs thyme leaf buds

In a small frying pan, combine pistachio nuts, red pepper, and diced bacon; sauté for 3 minutes and set aside.

Clean chicken breasts very well, then dice the meat and season with salt, white pepper, and mustard powder.

Using ice, chill the bucket of a food processor. Add seasoned chicken. Begin to purée, and slowly add drops of cream. When all the cream is in, add the egg whites.

Transfer mixture to a bowl and fold in sautéed nuts, pepper, and bacon.

Stuff the hens with the chicken-and-nuts mixture, then roll each bird tightly and wrap in bacon slices. Place hens in an oven-proof roasting pan, season, then sprinkle with thyme leaf buds.

Bake at 350°F for 18 to 24 minutes, or until the juices run clean. Remove from oven and loosely cover with foil. Allow to rest.

Crisp for 5 minutes at 450°F just before cutting and serving.

To serve, cut each prepared hen into approximately half-inch slices, but keep the shape together, and arrange on a plate. Finish with the Natural Hen Sauce drizzled around the hen.

Stuffed Cornish Hen

Rum-Spiked Jerk Chicken

I love Jamaican foods and classic Jamaican jerk. Instead of traditional jerk I use my own Black Spice Rub and finish things off with a rum glaze. You'll need to make Olaf's Black Spice Rub on page 189.

2 chicken breasts, boneless, cut into cubes
2 chicken legs, boneless, cut into cubes
1 cup Olaf's Black Spice Rub (page 189)
1 stalk sugar cane

Cover the chicken cubes with Olaf's Black Spice Rub, then refrigerate for an hour.

Cut the sugar-cane stalk into skewers; set aside the trimming to use in the glaze.

Divide the chicken into 4 servings and slide cubes on to skewers, alternating dark and white meat.

Rum Glaze

3/4 cup water
3/4 cup sugar
1/2 cup brown sugar
1 cup dark rum
1 tsp. pimento seeds, cracked
sugar cane, trimmings (from skewers)
3 tbsp. lime juice, or the juice from 2 limes
sea salt

In a small pot, combine water, sugar, rum, pimento, and cane trimmings from making your skewers. Place over medium-high heat and simmer for about 15 minutes or until the liquid has a syrup-like consistency.

Strain through a fine sieve into a clean pot.

On the barbecue, sear the skewers of chicken until chicken is fully cooked or the internal temperature reaches 165°F. Brush with the Rum Glaze.

To finish, place the skewers on a plate and spray with lime juice, then sprinkle with sea salt.

. . . .

Tip: All good jerk spiced foods love fresh lime juice and sea salt as a finish.

. . . .

Chicken Stuffed with Orange-Braised Duck

Duck, chicken, and orange—my version of Duck a l'Orange. You'll need to prepare two recipes for this dish: Sweet Orange Sauce, page 185, and Braised Duck Leg, page 191. Or you can use store-bought cooked duck.

Stuffing

1/4 cup unsalted butter
2 cups leek, finely diced
2 scallions, finely sliced
1/4 cup freshly sliced parsley
2 tbsp. thyme, chopped
1 lb. Braised Duck Leg, or store-bought barbecue duck
1 egg yolk
salt and black pepper to taste
1 cup fresh bread crumbs
2 tsp. orange zest, or the zest from 1 orange

In a pan, melt the butter and add in the leek. Sauté until tender. Add in the scallions, parsley, and thyme, then add roughly a quarter of the duck meat. Mix well.

Place warm mixture in a bowl. Add egg yolk and adjust seasoning.

Using a hand blender or food processor, quickly blend for just long enough to mix in the egg, leaving the mixture chunky. Don't overblend. You want visible chunks of duck.

Add the remaining shredded duck meat, bread crumbs, and orange zest. Using your hands, mix the ingredients thoroughly. The mixture should be dry but somewhat sticky to the touch.

Let the mixture cool.

Chicken

4 chicken breasts, 6 ounces each, skin on
1 recipe Sweet Orange Sauce (page 185)

Preheat the oven to 350°F.

On a cutting board covered with plastic wrap, place the breast, skin-side down, with the tenderloin (finger-like piece of flesh attached to the breast) flipped to one side.

Using a sharp knife, make a lengthwise slit down the middle of the breast, cutting about halfway into the breast. Open up the incision and make another slit on each side to form a pocket inside the breast.

Place a quarter of the stuffing into each chicken breast pocket. Close the pocket by folding in the sides and pulling the tenderloin back over to the middle.

Bake for 20 to 30 minutes, or until internal temperature is 170°F. Allow to rest for 10 minutes before cutting—this keeps all the juices inside.

Pour the Sweet Orange Sauce onto a warm plate and top with the chicken.

. . . .

Tip: Make sure stuffing mixture is well seasoned to ensure that the chicken breast has big flavors from the inside and out.

. . . .

All-Canadian Cheeseburger

I am proud to say I recently became a Canadian citizen. As a result I felt the need to do my own version of the Banquet Burger that is served at the CNE. Wave those flags everyone!

The Patties

1 lb. AAA Canadian beef, ground chuck regular
1 tsp. sea salt
1 tsp. black pepper

In a medium bowl, combine all ingredients together without overworking the mixture. Divide into 4 equal portions and press into patties, ensuring there are no air pockets. Cover and chill in the refrigerator.

Topping

8 oz. smoked pork
4 oz. double smoked bacon, cooked and diced
1 medium white onion, sliced and caramelized
6 oz. aged Cheddar, shredded
4 oz. soft Cheddar cheese spread
1 tsp. black pepper
4 big burger buns

In a medium bowl, combine all ingredients except the buns and set aside.

Preheat the grill to 400°F. Cook the burger for 4 to 6 minutes on each side, or until the internal temperature reaches 165°F.

During the last minute of cooking, pile on the topping mixture about one inch thick. Continue cooking until the topping has melted.

. . . .

Tip: For ultimate flavor, my first choice of ground beef is regular ground chuck with a fat content of approximately 21 to 23%.

. . . .

Beef Wellington Burger

A signature dish at my Ten Restaurant & Wine Bar. A sure winner at your next barbecue! Take my word for it. You'll need to make the Port Wine Reduction on page 186.

The Patties

1 lb. AAA Canadian beef, ground chuck regular
1 tsp. fresh ground black pepper
1 tsp. sea salt
12 oz. AAA Canadian beef fillet

Start off by placing ground beef chuck in a bowl. Add fresh ground pepper and mix well. Form into four equal balls, making sure to push all air out of the meat. Press the balls down to form perfect round patties.

Refrigerate, then season with salt just before grilling.

Slice the beef fillet in long strips; you want them to resemble bacon. Season well with salt and pepper.

Wellington Topping

12 oz. mushrooms (white, shiitake, oyster), sliced
2 oz. olive oil
2 oz. butter
1 clove garlic, minced
1/2 cup sliced shallots
1 sprig rosemary, finely chopped
1 sprig thyme, finely chopped
salt and pepper
4 sprigs Italian flat leaf parsley, finely sliced
6 oz. aged white Cheddar, grated

In a large frying pan on high heat, heat olive oil and sear mushrooms until golden brown in color.

Add in the butter, garlic, shallots, rosemary, and thyme and continue to sauté. Season well with salt and pepper. Transfer the mushroom mixture to a bowl, add in parsley and aged cheddar, then mix well.

When the mixture is at room temperature, form it into four patties and refrigerate.

Assembly

1 recipe Port Wine Reduction (page 186)
4 hamburger buns

Grill the burger patties 3 minutes per side, or until they're medium. Set to side of grill. Sear beef fillet strips to medium rare and remove from the grill.

Reduce the heat on the grill and baste the burger patties with half of the Port Wine Reduction. Top the patties with the mushroom mixture and close the lid of the grill. Allow mushroom mixture to melt into beef patties. Heat until the internal temperature of the beef is 165°F.

Remove from grill and transfer to buns.

. . . .

Tip: When you sauté the mushrooms, they will get quite watery before they become golden brown. This is normal: mushrooms are mostly made up of water.

. . . .

Beef Fillet Wrapped in Herb Collar

Beef tenderloin is probably the greatest cut of beef you can buy.

It is terrific for basic steak recipes, but I have dressed it up with

a collar of flavor and a variety of textures. Beef Wellington, take

a step back.

Beef Fillet

4 6-oz. beef tenderloin fillets
salt and pepper

Preheat the oven to 350°F.

Season the fillets on both sides with salt and pepper.

In a large frying pan, over medium-high heat, sear the beef fillets on all sides. Place them in the oven and continue to cook until the internal temperature is 125°F. Place the fillets on a warm plate, tent with tin foil, and allow to rest.

Herb Collar

5 cups fresh white bread crumbs
1 head roasted garlic
1 tbsp. rosemary, chopped
1 tbsp. thyme, chopped
1 tbsp. parsley, sliced
1/2 cup olive oil
1/2 tsp. sea salt
1/2 tsp. cracked black pepper
2 egg yolks

In a small bowl, combine all ingredients until you have a dough-like mixture. Cover and refrigerate for at least an hour.

Place the herb crust between two sheets of parchment paper and roll out until the dough is 1/4-inch in thickness. Cut into one-inch-wide strips. Remove layers of parchment paper, then wrap herb collar strips around the fillets and place in a baking pan. Bake for 5 minutes, or until the internal temperature of the beef is 135°F.

Onion Relish

1/4 cup olive oil
1 large sweet onion, minced
1 sprig thyme
1 bay leaf
3/4 cup sugar
1/2 cup herb vinegar
2 cups water
salt and pepper to taste

In a medium pot, over medium heat, heat the olive oil and sauté the onion, thyme, and bay leaf. Slowly add the sugar, vinegar, and water.

Reduce liquid by 80% or until mixture has a relish-like consistency. Season with salt and pepper; remove the bay leaf and thyme sprig.

Place fillets on plates and top with relish.

. . . .

Tip: The technique of reducing a finely diced vegetable or fruit gives you a very versatile recipe. Feel free to switch up the ingredients. I always do!

. . . .

My Ribs...My Home-Brewed BBQ Sauce

Fall-off-the-bone braised ribs with homemade barbecue sauce.

You'll need to mix up a batch of the BBQ Sauce on page 188.

Great food made from scratch with lots of love.

3 lbs. baby back pork ribs
1 cup brown sugar
1 tbsp. ancho chili powder
1/3 cup salt
2 tbsp. smoked paprika
1 tbsp. black pepper
1/4 cup garlic flakes
3 onions, sliced
6 cloves garlic, sliced
2 bay leaves
1 tbsp. cracked pepper
4 cups chicken stock.
1 recipe BBQ Sauce (page 188)

Score the underside of the back ribs with a sharp knife.

Place brown sugar, chili powder, 1/3 cup salt, paprika, pepper, and garlic flakes in a blender or food processor and mix until combined.

Rub mixture all over the ribs, then place ribs in a metal or glass dish. Cover with plastic wrap and chill for 24 hours.

Preheat oven to 325°F.

In a deep oven dish, place sliced onion, sliced garlic, bay leaves, and pepper. Place the ribs on top; pour in chicken stock.

Cover the ribs with parchment paper, then aluminum foil, and seal the foil around the pan. Bake for 1 3/4 hours, or until the meat comes cleanly off the bone. Cool the ribs and cut into portions.

Reheat in the oven or, even better, on the barbecue, brushing with BBQ Sauce just before serving. Serve extra sauce on the side for dipping.

Braised Meals

Braised Meals

When she wasn't at the market, my Oma was in the kitchen nursing a large pot of food that would take hours to cook. Whatever came out of the pot was fantastic and somehow managed to keep feeding more and more people. Needless to say, this chapter is all about my Oma's *wunderbar* one-pot creations.

I try to make these dishes even better by using modern technology, ingredients, and techniques to twist and refine great staples into classic foods. Back in the day, cooks slaved over their dishes and nurtured them to perfection. Keep in mind that these recipes are based on tradition; expect to put a little labor into them.

One-Big-Pot Dishes

One-Big-Pot Dishes

Smoked Pork and Carrot Stew

This old-school German comfort food is my Oma's most asked-for dish. Eating this makes me happy, happy, happy.

Smoked Pork and Carrot Stew

1/2 cup vegetable oil
1 lb. smoked pork, cut into cubes
2 white onions, diced
2 lbs. carrots, cut into 1-inch pieces
1/4 cup honey
2 sprigs thyme, chopped
2 yellow-flesh potatoes, diced
6 cups vegetable stock
1 bay leaf
4 carrots, juiced
salt and pepper to taste
1/4 cup flat-leaf parsley, sliced
1/4 cup chives, sliced
1/4 cup chervil leaves

In a large pot over medium heat, heat the oil and sauté the pork until golden brown. Add the onions and continue to sauté until translucent. Add the carrots and cook for 5 minutes.

Add the honey, thyme, and potatoes. Sauté for 5 minutes. Add the vegetable stock and bay leaf. Reduce the liquid by 50% and add the carrot juice. Bring to a simmer and adjust the seasoning.

Purée 1/3 of the cooked carrot pieces and return to the stew.

Add the parsley, chives, and chervil just before serving.

. . . .

Tip: Be wary of seasoning with too much salt. The smoked pork in this dish has a fair bit of salt that will flavor the stew throughout the cooking process.

. . . .

If you don't have a juicer, you can purchase bottled carrot juice. I would prefer that you place raw finely diced vegetables into a blender, add cold water to cover, and blend until liquefied.

Veal Paprikash

I was lucky enough, in 1988, to take part in a culinary exchange

between Berlin and Budapest. Part of the thrill of this experience

was the different dishes the Executive Chef prepared every day.

Of all the recipes, this is the one that continues to fill my head

with memories of Hungary.

1/2 cup oil
1 1/2 lbs. veal tenderloin, cut into 1-inch pieces
4 large onions, diced
2 cloves garlic, chopped
salt and black pepper
3 tbsp. Hungarian paprika
1 tsp. cayenne pepper
3 vine-ripened tomatoes, finely chopped
1 tbsp. caraway seeds
4 tbsp. flour
2 cups red wine
8 cups light beef stock
1 tsp. orange zest, or the zest from half an orange
1 tsp. lemon zest, or the zest from half a lemon
1 bay leaf
1 tbsp. chopped marjoram
1/4 cup sour cream

Heat the oil in a large pot over medium-high heat. Sear the veal pieces and brown on all sides. Reduce heat to medium and add the onion and garlic. Sauté until onion is golden brown. Season well and add the paprika, cayenne pepper, tomatoes, caraway seeds, and flour.

Add the red wine, reduce liquid by 80%, then add the beef stock and slowly simmer for 45 to 60 minutes. Add the zest, bay leaf, and marjoram.

Add salt and pepper to taste. Simmer an additional 5 minutes. Stir in the sour cream and serve immediately.

• •

Tip: For extra smoothness, remove the veal when it has finished cooking, stir in the sour cream then strain through a sieve. Don't reheat the stew once the sour cream has been added, as the cream could curdle. Fold the veal back into the finished sauce.

• •

Veal in Horseradish and Gooseberries

This one was taught to me by my Opa in Berlin. He was a great cook, as was his brother. This recipe is my new version of beef and horseradish. Instead of being roasted, the meat is poached in a creamy horseradish sauce. The sweet yet tart gooseberries give this dish a twist that makes it just incredible.

8 cups very rich chicken stock
1/4 cup salt
2 bay leaves
3 cloves garlic, sliced
1 tsp. cracked peppercorns
1/4 cup thyme
12 mini potatoes
3 carrots, cut into large dice
4 celery stalks, cut into large dice
1 1/2 lbs. veal tenderloin
1/3 cup butter
1/3 cup flour
1 cup whipping cream
1/2 cup sour cream
horseradish, to taste
2 tbsp. lemon juice, or the juice from half a lemon
seasoning
1 cup chives, sliced
1 pint green gooseberries

In a large pot bring the stock, salt, bay leaves, pepper, and thyme to a boil.

Poach the potatoes, carrots, and celery until tender. Using a slotted spoon, remove the vegetables from the stock; set aside and keep warm.

Set the veal tenderloin in the simmering stock, reduce the heat to low, and simmer for approximately 12 minutes, or until the internal temperature of the meat is 135°F. Remove tenderloin from pot, transfer to a plate, cover, and keep warm.

In a small pot over medium heat, melt the butter. Add in the flour, 3 cups of poaching stock, and the whipping cream; whisk into a smooth sauce. Simmer for 15 minutes to cook the flour. Remove from the heat and stir in the sour cream, horseradish, and lemon juice. Salt and pepper to taste.

To serve, fold in the chives and gooseberries. Scoop vegetables and a generous serving of sauce on a warm dinner plate and top with the tenderloin.

Tip: Making sure this broth is incredibly strong and well-seasoned will infuse the vegetables, potatoes, and veal with bold flavor.

Soured Beef Short Ribs

My Oma always made this dish with dumplings. Be warned that she would be very disappointed with anyone who doesn't give these savory beef ribs a try. This combination of savory, sweet, and sour is to die for. You'll need to start this meal the day before you serve it, as the ribs marinate for twenty-four hours. You can make the garnish while the ribs are baking.

Soured Beef Short Ribs

Ribs and Marinade

1 1/2 lb. Frenched beef short ribs
4 cups red wine
2 cups red wine vinegar
2 cups water
2 onions, sliced
6 bay leaves
1 tbsp. cracked black peppercorns
1 tbsp. mustard seed

Place the short ribs in a single layer in a deep glass dish. Combine all remaining ingredients and pour over ribs. Cover and refrigerate for 24 hours.

Garnish

1/4 cup herbal schnapps
1/4 cup golden sultana raisins
1/4 cup almonds
1/4 cup honey
2 cups pumpernickel bread crumbs, fine
1 tbsp. thyme, chopped
1 tbsp. savory, sliced

Warm the schnapps, add the raisins, and let soak for 30 minutes.

In a small pan over medium-high heat, toast the almonds, watching carefully to avoid burning them. Add the honey and raisins and reduce liquid to a syrup-like consistency.

When the ribs are tender, carefully transfer them to a serving platter, reserving baking liquid. Cover ribs with foil to keep warm.

Strain the baking liquid into a medium pot and skim off the excess fat. Over medium heat, simmer to reduce until liquid is the consistency of a sauce.

Thicken the sauce with the pumpernickel crumbs and adjust the seasoning if necessary.

Top the ribs with the chopped thyme and sliced savory.

• •

Tip: Time permitting, it is much easier to remove the fat from the sauce if you let it cool; the fat will rise to the surface and harden.

• •

Vegetables

1/2 cup oil
1 small onion, diced
1 clove garlic, sliced
2 parsley roots, chopped
1 tsp. fresh ginger root, minced
1 tsp. thyme, chopped
3 bay leaves
1/4 cup red wine vinegar
6 cups dry red wine
salt and pepper to taste
8 cups beef stock
4 juniper berries

Preheat the oven to 350°

Remove the meat from the marinade. In a deep oven-safe pan over high heat, add 1/4 cup of the oil and sear the ribs until dark brown on all sides. Remove the ribs and set aside.

Add the rest of the oil to the pan, then sauté onion, garlic, parsley root, ginger, thyme, and bay leaves until onion is golden brown. Pour in the red wine vinegar and deglaze.

Add the wine and ribs. Season. Bring liquid to a simmer. Add the beef stock and juniper berries, cover, and transfer pan to the oven. Bake for 2 hours.

Beef Roll-Ups
with Tomato Fondue Sauce

This is one of my best go-to dishes. When I was a young chef in a popular Italian restaurant, this recipe was a hair away from signature-dish status.

Beef Roll-Ups

1 red pepper
1 zucchini
1 eggplant
1 red onion
1 cup olive oil
salt and pepper
1 1/4 lbs. beef tenderloin fillet

Slice the vegetables in long one-inch strips and toss in oil, salt, and pepper. In a deep frying pan or on the barbecue, quickly fry or roast the vegetables. Place on a paper towel to remove any excess oil.

Cut the tenderloin into four portions of two-inch rounds. Laying the tenderloin portion on its side, flat side down, coming from the top of the roll, cut into the meat about one-inch, then turning the knife, and while rolling the tenderloin, cut the meat into a spiral that when unrolled will give you a rectangle of meat, ready to take the vegetables. The idea is to end up with a long, flat strip.

Take one of each vegetable, place them all at the end of a tenderloin strip and roll it up until tightly wrapped. Repeat with the other three portions.

In a large pan over medium-high heat, sear the tenderloin. Reduce to medium heat and continue to cook for approximately 5 minutes. Remove from the pan and allow to rest.

Tomato Sauce

3 tbsp. olive oil
1 clove garlic, sliced
10 basil leaves
5 shallots, finely minced
1 lb. vine-ripened tomatoes, diced
1 tsp. sugar
1 tbsp. butter, cold, cut into cubes
salt and pepper to taste

In a small pot, over medium heat, heat the olive oil and sauté the garlic and half the basil leaves for a few minutes. Add the shallots and tomatoes and simmer for 10 minutes over medium-low heat. Add the sugar.

In a food processor or blender, place the tomato mixture and purée until there are no large lumps. Pour back into the pot by passing through a fine sieve, then whisk in the cold butter and remaining basil leaves. Season to taste with salt and pepper.

Place the stuffed fillet of beef into the middle of a plate and spoon the sauce around the fillet.

. . . .

Tip: The key to this dish is not overcooking it. It is better to undercook it a little and allow the meat to cook to perfection while it is resting.

. . . .

Smoked Turkey Thighs with Lentils and Pea Pesto

A modern take on an old-world classic. I have managed to lighten up a dish without compromising its integrity by substituting turkey for smoked pork. It is advisable to soak the lentils in cold water for about 3 hours prior to cooking them.

Lentils

2 cups dry red lentils
1 carrot, finely diced
1 celery stalk, finely diced
1/2 cup olive oil
2 small onions, finely diced
1 clove garlic, minced
1/2 cup tomato paste
2 cups herb vinegar
2 sprigs fresh thyme
4 cups chicken or vegetable stock
1 bay leaf
salt and white pepper to taste

Soak lentils in cold water for three hours.

Set aside half the diced carrot and celery.

In a medium pot heat the olive oil and sauté the onion, garlic, half the carrot, and half the celery. Add the tomato paste, vinegar, lentils, and thyme then simmer for 3 minutes.

Add the chicken stock and bay leaf. Simmer about 20 minutes. Taste and adjust the seasonings.

Fold in the reserved carrots and celery.

Smoked Turkey Thighs

4 cooked smoked turkey thighs
1/4 cup sliced sage
salt and pepper
2 tsp. lemon zest, or the zest of half a lemon

Preheat oven to 275°F. Place the turkey thighs in a roasting pan and season with sage, salt, pepper, and lemon zest. Roast for approximately 30 minutes.

Pea Pesto

2 cups fresh green peas
1/2 cup sour cream
2 cloves garlic, minced
1/2 cup onion, minced
1/2 cup mint, sliced
1/2 cup parsley, sliced
salt and pepper to taste
1/2 cup olive oil

To a food processor or blender, add all ingredients except olive oil, and purée. Slowly drizzle in the olive oil while continuing to purée.

In the middle of the plate, spoon a generous portion of lentils. On top of the lentils, place a crispy smoked turkey thigh and finish off with a spoon of the Pea Pesto.

Serve at room temperature.

• •

Tip: Heating the turkey for longer at low heat will result in golden crispy skin and meat that falls off the bone.

• •

Turkey Thigh Osso Buco

When we think of osso buco we all think of veal. I think it's time to start using turkey and I'm starting with the thigh. Turkey turns classic, rich, Italian osso buco into a light simmered dish, and it comes with its own special gremolata.

1/2 cup olive oil
4 turkey thighs, natural or smoked
6 cloves garlic, sliced
1 cup basil, sliced
1/4 cup oregano, chopped
1 onion, finely diced
1 cup celery root, finely diced
1 cup carrots, finely diced
1 cup celery, finely diced
2 bay leaves
4 cups dry white wine
8 medium plum tomatoes
6 cups chicken stock
1/4 cup sugar
1/4 cup sage, sliced
1/4 cup savory, sliced
salt and pepper to taste

Preheat oven to 350°F.

In a large oven-proof pan over medium heat, heat the olive oil and sear the turkey thighs until golden on all sides. Add the garlic, basil, oregano, and onion and sauté for 3 minutes.

Toss in the vegetables and continue to sauté for another 5 minutes. Add the bay leaves and deglaze with the wine. Reduce liquid by 80% then add the tomatoes, chicken stock, and sugar. Cover and bake in the oven for one hour, or until internal temperature of the meat is 165°F. Remove the turkey and some of the vegetables and set aside. Take the remaining tomato and vegetable mixture and purée into a smooth sauce.

Combine everything and season with salt and pepper to taste. Let the turkey and vegetables rest while you prepare the gremolata.

Gremolata

2 cups parsley, sliced
3 tbsp. lemon juice, or the juice of 1 lemon
2 tsp. lemon zest, or the zest of 1 lemon
3 tbsp. orange juice, or the juice of 1 orange
2 tsp. orange zest, or the zest of 1 orange
1 sprig thyme, chopped
4 cloves garlic, minced
3/4 cup olive oil
salt and pepper to taste

Place all ingredients except the oil, salt, and pepper in a food processor and chop. Slowly drizzle in the olive oil then adjust the seasoning to taste.

To serve, plate the braised vegetables and tomato sauce, top with the turkey, and garnish with gremolata.

• •

Tip: Orange zest is an unexpectedly wonderful addition to tomato sauces. Try it and you'll really taste how it enhances the flavor.

• •

Turkey Thigh Osso Buco

Curried Chicken

My friend Sandeep is a culinary exchange student from India. He has recently become part of my kitchen team. When asked for his input, Sandeep opted to contribute a recipe that is straight from the heart. This is his family's recipe for curried chicken.

1 1/2 lbs. chicken thighs, cut into 1-inch cubes
1/2 tsp. ground cumin
1 tbsp. paprika
1/2 tsp. cayenne pepper
1/2 tsp. ground cardamom
1 tbsp. fennel seeds, crushed
1/2 tsp. ground coriander
1/4 tsp. turmeric
salt and pepper to taste
2 tbsp. vegetable oil
1 cup yogurt

Set aside half the spices. In a large bowl, combine half the spices with all of the yogurt and oil then add the chicken pieces. Cover and marinate in the refrigerator for 6 hours.

Sauce

1 clove garlic, chopped
1 tsp. ginger root, grated
1 red onion, chopped
1/4 cup oil
3 large vine-ripened tomatoes, chopped
2 tbsp. cashew nut paste
1 cup whipping cream
2 cups chicken stock
1/4 bunch fresh coriander, sliced
1/2 cup butter, cold, cut into cubes

In a medium pot over medium heat, sauté the garlic, ginger, and onion in oil until golden brown. Add reserved spice mixture and toast for 1 minute. Add the tomatoes and cashew nut paste. Bring to a boil and simmer for 10 minutes, stirring occasionally. Add the cream, chicken stock, and coriander, and adjust seasoning to taste.

Put the mixture into a food processor or blender and purée until smooth.

Pour pureé into a medium pot, add the cooked chicken pieces, and simmer over medium-high heat for 10 minutes, then add the puréed sauce.

Simmer for an additional 10 minutes, then whisk in the cold butter cubes.

. . . .

Tip: Toasting spices in a dry frying pan for a few minutes before you add them to a recipe makes a big difference.

. . . .

Save Water, Use Beer!

Save Water, Use Beer!

We have all heard that nothing goes better with fine food than fine wine. Well, things have changed, and fine beer is taking its place alongside some wonderful dishes—it's even great for cooking with.

Beers offer a variety of tastes and flavors that can enhance some dishes by creating more depth. Stews, ragouts, marinated meats, fish, chocolate, cheese, and fruits are all things that have enormous potential when combined with beer. Any chef will help you pair wines with your meal, but at the end of a grueling day, guaranteed, the chef is having a cold one.

My passion for beer began about ten years ago when I met John and Julie Sleeman and a very important friendship developed. This was the start of a beautiful thing—the beer maker and the cook, what a perfect match.

I started cooking private dinners for the Sleemans and began challenging myself to take John's prize beer and use it as an ingredient in my creations. I graduated from beef dishes and moved on to fish, pork, poultry, and desserts. I recently opened West 50, which is the largest draft beer house in Canada. The menu there is largely infused with beer inspiration.

Wherever I used to cook with water or wine, I now find it extremely fun to get creative with beer. Just remember, beer loves food and food loves beer.

Beer Cuisine

Beer Cuisine

Spicy Stout Beer Garlic Shrimp ...132

Mussels and Smoked Salmon in Wheat Beer ...133

Smoked Trout with Wheat Beer Sabayon ...135

Beer-Brined Roast Chicken ...136

Smoked Pork Baked in Beer Rye Bread ...138

Festive Ham with Maple Stout and Brat Apple Marmalade ...140

Drunken Soya Glazed Ribs ...142

Spicy Stout Beer Garlic Shrimp

You have all had garlic shrimp. Add the malt aromas of stout

beer and a hint of selected spices and WOW!

20 large shrimp, deveined, cleaned, and butterflied
2 tbsp. olive oil
6 cloves garlic, minced
1 small onion, minced
1 red chili, sliced
2 cups dark stout beer
1/2 cup tomato sauce
salt and white pepper to taste
4 scallions, finely sliced
1 tbsp. butter, cold, cut into cubes

In a large frying pan on medium heat, quickly sauté the shrimp in the olive oil for 2 minutes until medium rare. Remove shrimp from pan. Using the flavors already in the pan, sauté the garlic, onion, and red chili until onion is light brown. Deglaze with beer, then add the tomato sauce. Simmer 3 minutes, then add seasonings. Return the shrimp to the pan. Add the scallions and whisk in the cold butter cubes.

Pile five shrimp on top of each other on each plate, then cover with the sauce.

· ·

Tip: Make sure you remove the shrimp after 2 minutes of cooking to ensure they don't overcook and become rubbery. Make the sauce, then fold the shrimp into the hot sauce and serve immediately.

· ·

Mussels and Smoked Salmon in Wheat Beer

This has all the makings for a romantic night. Just add

candlelight—and more beer.

1/4 cup olive oil
4 lbs. fresh P.E.I. mussels
1 clove garlic, minced
1 small onion, minced
4 oz. smoked salmon
salt and white pepper to taste
2 cups wheat beer
1 tsp. Dijon mustard
salt to taste
1 tsp. hot pepper sauce
1 cup whipping cream, whipped
1/4 cup tarragon, sliced
1/4 cup parsley, sliced
1 tsp. lemon juice

In cold water, wash and scrub mussels, then remove beards. Discard any mussels that are broken or open. In a large pot, heat the oil and sauté the mussels, garlic, onion, and smoked salmon. Season with a little salt and white pepper. Add one cup of the beer and cover pot. Steam just until mussels open. Discard any that do not open during steaming. Strain the mussels through a fine mesh strainer; save liquid. Set mussels aside.

To make the sauce, combine mustard and salt in a small pot. Whisk until smooth and light. Add the second cup of beer, hot pepper sauce, whipped cream, and 2 tbsp. strained mussel liquid. Place over medium heat and cook, whisking constantly. When the mixture is thick and foamy, remove from heat. Stir in the tarragon, parsley, and lemon juice.

Place mussels on a large platter or bowl and pour the rich beer sauce over them.

. . . .

Tip: Fresh mussels are a must! Cook with the mussel liquid to get wonderful flavors.

. . . .

Smoked Trout with Wheat Beer Sabayon

I absolutely love smoked trout—especially trout that is smoked over apple wood. Can you say fantastic? This dish is all about texture. Apple jelly, crispy wafers, succulent trout, and a foam of Beer Sabayon.

Smoked Trout with Wheat Beer Sabayon

Beer Sabayon

1 shallot, minced
1 tsp. Dijon mustard
1 large egg
1/2 tsp. salt
1 cup stout beer
1 tsp. hot pepper sauce
1 tbsp. cracked peppercorns
1 tsp. lemon juice
salt and white pepper to taste

Combine shallot, mustard, egg, and salt in a stainless steel bowl. Whisk until smooth and light. Add the beer and hot pepper sauce. Place bowl over a pot of gently simmering water and cook by whisking constantly, until mixture is thick and foamy. Remove from heat. Season to taste with lemon juice, salt, and pepper.

Apple Beer Jelly

6 sheets gelatin
2 cups wheat beer
4 cups apple juice
1 apple, peeled, cored, cut into cubes
5 red radishes, sliced
1/2 cup chives, sliced
1/2 cup dill, chopped
1/2 cup red onion, diced
salt and pepper

In a small bowl of cold water, submerge and soak the sheets of gelatin to soften.

In a large pot, over low heat, bring beer and apple juice to a simmer. Add apple cubes and radish slices and quickly blanch. When tender, remove apples and radishes with a slotted spoon; set aside.

To the beer and apple juice, add the gelatin sheets and stir until dissolved. Add the blanched apple and radishes; then add chives, dill, and red onion. Salt and pepper to taste.

Pour the mixture into individual molds of choice, cover, and refrigerate.

Sour Cream Horseradish

1/2 cup sour cream
1/2 cup horseradish
1 lemon, juice and zest
salt and pepper to taste

In a small bowl, combine all ingredients; chill.

Assembly

1 slice rye bread, cut wafer thin and toasted in the oven
1 small onion, very finely sliced
6 oz. smoked trout, sliced
dill sprigs, for garnish

Remove the jelly from the molds by dipping the molds in hot water for just a few seconds.

Place each jelly on a plate; top with a rye bread wafer, a spoonful of finely sliced onion, a few slices of smoked trout, and a spoonful of Sour Cream Horseradish; garnish each plate with a dill sprig.

To finish, spoon the Beer Sabayon around the jelly moulds to complete the plate.

• •

Tip: You can tell that the Sabayon has been whisked enough when it turns light yellow (almost white) in color.

• •

Beer-Brined Roast Chicken

Instead of sitting down with a cold beer and cooked chicken, I

have combined the two into a chicken dish that will make your

guests sit up and take notice.

3 12 oz. bottles wheat beer
4 cups water
1/3 cup salt
6 bay leaves
2 cups thyme
2 lemons, sliced
3 oranges, sliced
1 cup garlic, crushed
1 large onion, sliced
2 tbsp. cracked black pepper
1 tbsp. brown sugar
1 roasting chicken, 2 to 3 pounds

In a large soup pot, combine all ingredients except the chicken.
Bring to a boil, then chill quickly.

Add the chicken to the cold brine, and chill for 8 hours.

Preheat the oven to 375°F.

Rinse the chicken in cold water and place it in a roasting pan.
Season lightly with salt and pepper. Roast for approximately 40
minutes, or until the internal temperature is 165°F.

· ·

Tip: The brine should be cold before you add the chicken; warm or hot brine will
close the chicken's pores, and flavors will not penetrate.

· ·

Smoked Pork Baked in Beer Rye Bread

This is an amazing brunch or picnic dish. It can be eaten hot or cold and is unique.

Bread and Pork

1 3/4 cups warm stout beer
1 tbsp. dry active yeast
2 cups all-purpose flour
1 1/2 cups rye flour
1 cup oatmeal
1 tsp. salt
1/2 cup caramelized onions
1 tbsp. caraway seeds
1 cup sauerkraut
1 cup sun-dried apples
1 lb. smoked pork loin
sea salt, for sprinkling

Preheat the oven to 375°F.

Pour warm stout beer into a small warmed bowl. Sprinkle dry yeast over the surface. Put in a warm place for about 5 minutes and allow to activate. The yeast should be foamy.

In a large mixing bowl, combine flours, oatmeal, salt, onion, caraway seeds, sauerkraut, and apples. Stir in foaming beer-yeast mixture.

Cover the bowl with a clean cloth, place in a warm place away from any drafts, and let rise until doubled in size. This should take approximately one-hour.

When dough has risen, pound it down and place on a floured surface. Press out to a rectangle large enough to wrap around the pork loin.

Place the pork loin in the center of the dough, wrap it up, and press edges of dough to seal. Place seam-side down on a greased cookie sheet, cover with the clean cloth, and place in a warm place until dough has doubled in size.

Sprinkle the top of the loaf with sea salt and bake for 45 minutes. As the loaf bakes, spray surface with cold water at least twice, so a firm crust forms.

Remove loaf from the oven and allow to rest for at least one hour.

Beer Mustard

1 tbsp. oil
1 cup white onion, finely diced
1 cup mustard seeds
1/2 cup dry mustard powder
2 cups wheat beer
1/4 cup white vinegar
3 cups Dijon mustard

In a medium pot over medium heat, heat the oil and sauté onion until translucent. Add the mustard seeds, mustard powder, wheat beer, and white vinegar. Reduce liquid by 50%. Remove from heat and whisk in the Dijon mustard.

. . . .

Tip: The trick to yeast is warm liquid that is not too hot. The yeast must completely dissolve in the liquid, and a light froth should form on top.

. . . .

Smoked Pork Baked in Beer Rye Bread

Festive Ham
with Maple Stout
and Brat Apple Marmalade

This one is so easy. It's perfect for giving you time to visit with your guests or take part in some family festivities. Your guests will gasp when this ham is presented at the table. It's a true holiday feast.

The Ham

1 smoked ham loin, 4 pounds, with skin

Dry Rub

1/2 cup salt
1/4 cup pepper
1 tbsp. ground cloves
1 tbsp. cinnamon

Mix all ingredients together. Set aside.

Preheat the oven to 325°F.

Score the skin of the ham roast in one-inch diamonds then rub in all the Dry Rub. Place ham in a roasting pan and bake for 1 1/2 hours, or until an internal temperature reaches 145°F.

While ham is roasting, prepare Maple Stout Sauce, Brat Apple Marmalade, and Glaze.

Maple Stout Sauce

1/4 cup vegetable oil
4 cloves garlic, sliced
1 cup shallots, diced
12 oz. stout beer
1 cup balsamic vinegar
3/4 cup maple syrup
1 tbsp. rosemary, chopped
1 tbsp. thyme, chopped
1 tbsp. Dijon mustard
salt to taste

In a medium pot, heat the oil and slow-roast the garlic and shallots until golden brown.

Add the beer, vinegar, and maple syrup and simmer for 15 to 20 minutes, or until sauce reaches a syrupy consistency.

Remove from heat and add the herbs. Stir in the mustard and add salt to taste. Set aside in a warm place.

Brat Apple Marmalade

2 cups dark rum
1/2 cup golden sultana raisins
1 lb. baking apples, peeled, cored, and cut into
    large cubes
1 cinnamon stick
1 cup white sugar
1 cup brown sugar
1/2 cup whole almonds with skins, roasted and
    coarsely chopped
1 vanilla bean, split and scraped
3 tbsp. lemon juice, or the juice from 1 lemon
2 tsp. lemon zest, or the zest from 1 lemon

In a small pan, heat the rum until warm, remove from heat, add the raisins, and soak for about 15 minutes.

Meanwhile, in a large frying pan over high heat, sear the apple cubes until browned.

Add the cinnamon stick and sauté for 3 minutes.

Add and caramelize the white sugar.

Add the brown sugar, rum-soaked raisins, toasted almond, vanilla, lemon juice, and zest. The result will be a chunky, syrupy apple chutney. Set aside and keep warm.

Glaze

1 cup beetroot-sugar syrup or molasses
1/2 cup rum
1/2 cup apple juice
2 tbsp. thyme, chopped

Mix all ingredients together.

When roast has cooked for 1 1/2 hours or has reached an internal temperature of 145°F, brush with the glaze and return to the oven for an additional 10 minutes. Remove from the oven and glaze again. Serve ham with dollop of marmalade and Maple Stout Sauce pooled on the plate.

. . . .

Tip: The glaze has a high sugar content. It's important to add it at the last minute so it doesn't burn. Just before the roast goes to the table, brush it one more time to shine it up.

. . . .

You can also add this marmalade to baked cheeses—talk about delicious!

Drunken Soya Glazed Ribs

Pork ribs soaked in beer and Asian soy flavors make a great,

sticky mess that's perfect for sinking your teeth into.

The Ribs

2 tbsp. black pepper
1/4 cup salt
1 tbsp. curry
2 tbsp. Szechuan pepper
2 tbsp. coriander seeds
1 tbsp. brown sugar
2 lbs. pork side riblets, split lengthwise, membrane cut

Preheat oven to 325°F.

In a blender or food processor, blend the pepper, salt, curry, Szechuan pepper, coriander seeds, and brown sugar until well mixed. Rub this mixture onto the riblets. Set aside.

Soy Purée

1/2 tsp. sesame seed oil
12 cloves garlic
2 onions
1/4 cup ginger
3 oranges juice and zest
4 cups soy sauce
4 cups stout beer

Without cleaning the food processor, add all Soy Purée ingredients and purée.

Pour half the purée into a 3-inch-deep roasting pan, place the riblets on top, and cover with the remaining purée.

Cover top of pan with parchment paper, then seal with a layer of foil.

Bake for 1 1/2 hours, or until the meat can be pulled cleanly away from the bone. Remove ribs from pan and keep warm.

Strain liquid from the roasting pan into a medium-size pot and reduce to 2 cups.

Finishing Sauce

1/4 cup honey
1 tbsp. sesame seeds
1/2 cup scallions, sliced
1/2 cup coriander leaves, sliced
salt and pepper to taste
1 cup roasted peanuts, crushed

Add all ingredients to the 2 cups of braising liquid.

Cut the ribs between each bone so that they are bite-size. In a large frying pan, over high heat, toss the riblets to reheat them, then brown for 3 minutes. Toss with Finishing Sauce and serve.

· ·

Tip: When buying ribs, make sure the tops of the ribs are very meaty. Ask your butcher to split the ribs down the length for bite-size pieces.

· ·

The New Pre-dessert

Cheese is, outright, the new shining-star ingredient in any trendy, cutting-edge kitchen. The greatest raw ingredient in the whole world is cheese! Every country, town, or village has a cheese that they profess is probably the best. There are seven categories or levels of cheeses, ranging from soft and mild to firm, hard, and pungent. In my opinion, the stinkier the better.

You can do a cheese tasting with a range of flavors and textures that builds in intensity. When tasting cheeses, try chewing them a little and enjoy letting them melt in your mouth like you would chocolate. There is nothing better than trying cheeses with a variety of accompaniments such as fruits, nuts, wine, or beer. Once you have eaten some distinct cheeses, you will certainly want to incorporate them into hot baked dishes.

Here are some fantastic dishes for your next get-together. Consider replacing sweet desserts with a hot, savory cheese course. It's a different finish to a great evening. Don't be afraid to enjoy the most sinful of all the food groups!

The New Pre-dessert

Cheese Courses

Baked Saganaki
with Date and Fig Salad

My inspiration from Greece! I just can't say enough about Greek food. The ingredients are always light, simple, fresh, and never masked by overly heavy sauces. My holiday in Greece continues to influence my cooking to this day.

Date and Fig Salad

2 cups dates, pitted and chopped
2 cups figs, quartered
1 tbsp. anise seeds, toasted
1 tbsp. lemon juice, or the juice from half a lemon
1 tsp. lemon zest, or the zest from half a lemon
2 oz. ouzo
1/2 cup walnut pieces, toasted
1 cup green grapes, seedless
1 tbsp. honey

Combine all the ingredients together and set aside.

Crispy Saganaki

1 egg
1 cup whole milk
1/2 cup flour
1/2 cup fresh bread crumbs
3/4 lb. Kasseri cheese, cut into 4 pieces
1/2 cup olive oil
2 oz. brandy
2 lemons, halved
4 rounds pita bread

In a shallow bowl, combine egg and milk. Put the flour bread-crumb mixture into another bowl. Dip the cheese pieces first into the egg wash, then into the flour-breading. Let sit for a few minutes to allow the flour-breading to dry onto the cheese pieces.

In a large nonstick frying pan over medium-high heat, heat the olive oil then very carefully place the floured cheese pieces into the oil; sauté until the coating is crispy. Remove the pieces from the oil with a slotted spoon and place on a paper towel to remove any excess oil.

Pour the oil from the pan into a container (the oil can be saved for frying at a later date). In the warm pan, place lemons, cut side down, and roast until lightly browned.

Now for your truly Greek presentation: place the crispy cheese pieces on a large plate, squeeze on the roasted lemon, pour on the brandy, then ignite it to flambé. Serve with warm pita bread and Date and Fig Salad. *Opa!*

. . . .

Tip: Make sure the olive oil for frying is hot enough so that the cheese fries quickly and doesn't get stuck to the bottom of the frying pan.

. . . .

Baked Saganaki with Date and fig Salad

Baked Brie and Roasted Apples

1/2 cup whipping cream
8 oz. cream cheese, room temperature
12 oz. Brie cheese ring, with rind
salt
cayenne pepper
nutmeg
2 large baking apples, peeled, cored, and cut into
    large cubes
1/4 tsp. allspice
1 tbsp. brown sugar
2 tbsp. bourbon whiskey
1 tbsp. honey
2 tbsp. lemon juice, or juice from half a lemon
crispy bread

In a small pot over medium heat, warm the cream then stir in the cream cheese. Whisk until blended and smooth.

Remove the rind from the Brie ring; set aside 4 ounces of Brie for the garnish. Cut the rest of the Brie into rough cubes to allow for faster melting.

Add the Brie into the cream-cheese mixture, then add salt, cayenne pepper, and nutmeg to taste.

Portion into individual oven-proof cups and place a piece of reserved Brie on top of each. Place on an oven-proof tray and set aside.

In a medium nonstick pot over high heat, sear and roast the apple pieces until caramelized on all sides. Dust with allspice and brown sugar.

Deglaze with bourbon, honey, and lemon juice. Remove pot from the heat.

Preheat the broiler and place tray of Brie mixture under the grill until the tops begin to bubble and turn a golden brown.

Serve with Roasted Apples and crispy bread.

. . . .

Tip: Use a good unwaxed baking apple—organic if at all possible. A baking apple will hold up to the roasting process better than an eating apple.

. . . .

Blue Cheese and Walnut Apple Bake with Peppered Honey

Rum Raisins

1/4 cup raisins
1/4 cup rum

In a small pot, heat the rum until warm; remove from heat, add raisins, and soak until soft and plump.

Peppered Honey

1 cup buckwheat honey
1 tsp. thyme
1 tsp. coarse black pepper
1 tsp. lemon zest, or zest from half a lemon

Walnut Stuffing

1/2 cup chopped walnuts
1/4 cup unsalted butter
1/2 cup blue cheese
1 tsp. chives, sliced
1 tsp. parsley, sliced
4 large baking apples

Preheat the oven to 325°F

In a small pot over medium-high heat, combine the honey, thyme, pepper, and lemon zest. Simmer for 3 minutes. Set aside.

In a small pan over medium heat, toast the walnut pieces until heated through. Stir in the butter, raisins, and rum. Remove from the heat, then add the blue cheese and herbs.

Remove the top third of each apple and hollow out the core with a spoon. Stuff the apples with the walnut mixture, place on a baking tray lined with parchment paper, and bake for at least 20 minutes, or until the apple flesh is tender when poked with a clean knife.

Place on a warmed plate and drizzle with Peppered Honey.

. . . .

Tip: Cut a thin slice from the bottom of each apple prior to stuffing and baking. This will help it sit straight when baking or plating. Keep the top third of the apple with the stem still attached and place it on top of the stuffed apple as a lid for the last few minutes of baking.

. . . .

Goat Cheese and Gouda Dip with Tomato Jam

An On the Curve favorite that combines goat cheese, hot chilies,

and sweet tomato jam to make a spicy, savory treat.

Goat Cheese and Gouda Dip

1/2 cup whipping cream
1/2 cup cream cheese, room temperature
1 cup goat cheese
1 cup Gouda cheese, grated
2 red chili peppers
1/2 cup olive oil
bread

Preheat the oven to 350°F

In a medium pot over medium heat, whisk the cream, cream cheese, and goat cheese together until smooth and creamy. Fold in 3/4 of the Gouda cheese and heat until Gouda has melted.

Portion the cheese mixture into 4 individual oven-proof dishes. Evenly distribute the remaining Gouda over the dishes and set aside.

In the food processor, purée the chili peppers and olive oil.

Tomato Jam

1 28 oz. can crushed Italian plum tomatoes
1/2 cup sugar
1/2 cup water
1/2 cup onions, minced
1 tsp. cinnamon
1 tbsp. basil, sliced
1 tbsp. oregano, chopped
6 tbsp. lemon juice, or the juice from 2 lemons
2 tsp. lemon zest, or the zest from 2 lemons
salt and pepper to taste

In a medium pot over medium-low heat, combine all ingredients. Bring to a boil, then simmer, stirring constantly, for 30 minutes, or until the tomatoes have a jam-like consistency.

Bake the prepared cheese dishes for 5 minutes, or place under the broiler for 2 minutes until golden brown and bubbling.

Drizzle the tops with hot chili oil and serve with bread and Tomato Jam.

. . . .

Tip: While simmering the jam it is important to stir constantly to prevent the jam from burning or sticking to the bottom of the pot.

. . . .

Pick-Up Sticks with Liquid Parmesan

This one is from my partner, Brian. It's a great starter to share

while waiting for the family to gather for dinner.

1 bunch basil
1/2 cup olive oil
1 small onion, minced
2 bay leaves
750 mL dry white wine
4 cups whipping cream
1 rind from Parmigiano Reggiano
4 oz. Parmigiano Reggiano, grated
1 loaf day-old Italian crusty bread
2 cloves garlic, crushed
1 cup oil
salt and pepper
1 tbsp. smoked paprika

Preheat the oven to 350°F.

Pull the leaves off the basil stems; set aside the leaves.

In a large pot over medium heat, heat the olive oil and sauté onion, bay leaves, basil stems, and rind for 5 minutes. Deglaze with the white wine, then reduce heat to low and allow the liquid to reduce by 90%.

Add the cream and cheese rind, and simmer until liquid is reduced by 50%. Strain through a fine sieve into a clean pot.

While still warm, whisk in the cheese.

Cut crusty bread into sticks, each 1 inch by 1 inch by 8 inches. Line a baking sheet with parchment paper. Spread bread sticks out on baking sheet.

In a small dish, combine garlic, oil, salt, and pepper. Using a pastry brush, paint the bread sticks with the garlic oil. Place in the oven and bake until they are lightly toasted but still soft on the inside.

To serve, spoon cheese sauce onto a warmed plate, arrange bread sticks on top, garnish with basil leaves, and sprinkle with smoked paprika.

. . . .

Tip: If you're not using the cream-and-cheese sauce immediately, strain the cream mixture and keep it warm, then add the cheeses just before serving.

. . . .

Gratin Cheese Fondue with Red Wine Hazelnut and Quince Relish

Drunken, red-wine-and-spice-braised fruit piled onto caramelized grilled cheese. This one is really different and well worth the work!

Red Wine Hazelnut and Quince Relish

1 cup chopped hazelnuts
2 quince, cored, cut into generous cubes
1 1/2 cups black cherry juice
1 cup buckwheat honey
4 cups Italian red wine
1 bay leaf
1 stick cinnamon
1 tsp. cardamom
1 orange, juice and zest
1 lemon, juice and zest
2 pears, cored, cut into generous cubes
2 plums, stones removed, cut into generous cubes

To a large pot over medium-high heat, add the hazelnuts and roast for 3 to 4 minutes. Add the quince and sauté for 5 minutes, or until quince is golden brown.

Reduce the heat to low, add all remaining ingredients except pears and plums, and simmer for 30 minutes, or until the quince pieces are tender.

Add the pears and plums and simmer until liquid has reduced to a marmalade consistency.

Gratin Cheese Fondue

1/4 cup olive oil
1 small onion, finely diced
1/2 bay leaf
1/4 tsp. cracked peppercorns
1 1/2 cups white wine
1 cup whipping cream
salt and pepper to taste
4 oz. Swiss cheese, grated
1 cup Gouda cheese, grated
1 loaf farmer's bread (or a crusty bread of your choice), sliced

In a small pot over medium heat, heat the oil and sauté the onion, bay leaf, and peppercorns for 3 minutes, or until the onions are translucent.

Deglaze with the white wine and simmer for 10 minutes.

Add the cream, salt, and pepper then strain through a fine sieve into a large pot.

While the mixture is still warm, stir in both cheeses.

Set oven to broil and move the top rack to the highest position. On a large baking sheet, place the bread slices and generously spoon on the cheese mixture so all the bread is covered. Place under a broiler until the cheese is bubbling and golden brown. Watch carefully so as not to burn.

Serve the Red Wine Hazelnut and Quince Relish as a side to the fondue.

. . . .

Tip: When you're cooking the Red Wine Hazelnuts and Quince, the fruit should be tender, but not mushy or overcooked.

. . . .

Goat Cheese Brûlé Cake

This cake is weird, wild, and wonderful. It is a combination that is not altogether common and must be tried by all goat cheese lovers.

Almond Pastry

5 egg whites
1/3 cup sugar
2 cups ground almonds
3/4 cup icing sugar
3/4 cup cake flour

Preheat the oven to 350°F.

In a large bowl, whisk the egg whites and sugar until stiff peaks form. Fold in the almonds, icing sugar, and flour.

Line a baking sheet with parchment paper. Using a 4-inch cookie cutter or glass, draw eight circles on the paper.

Pour the egg white and almond mixture into a pastry bag and pipe circles into the outlines on the parchment until they are all filled in. Bake for 20 minutes. Cool.

Goat Cheese Filling

6 sheets gelatin
1 egg
2 egg yolks
1/3 cup sugar
1/4 cup cream cheese
3/4 cup goat cheese, softened
2 cups whipping cream, whipped
2 tsp. lemon zest, or the zest of 1 lemon

Soak the gelatin sheets in cold water to soften to a jelly-like consistency.

In a double boiler, or a metal bowl that fits over a pot of boiling water, whisk the egg, egg yolks, and sugar until the sugar has dissolved and the mixture forms into soft peaks or ribbons.

Remove from the heat. Scoop the gelatin sheets out of the cold water and add to the sugar mixture. Whisk until the gelatin is dissolved. Let the mixture cool to room temperature, then fold in the cream cheese, goat cheese, whipped cream, and lemon zest.

Garnish

1 pint blueberries
1 cup brown sugar

Ouzo Raisins

1 cup golden sultana raisins
1 cup ouzo
1/2 cup honey

In a small pot over medium heat, warm the raisins in the ouzo. Simmer for 5 minutes then remove from the heat and set aside until raisins have cooled to room temperature.

Assembly

It's time to build your masterpiece. Slice the almond cakes twice horizontally to make three thin slices. Place the bottom slices onto serving plates. Spread with the Goat's Cheese Filling. Add the second slice of cake and top with filling. Add the top slice.

Spoon Goat's Cheese Filling onto the top slice and allow it to run over the sides, then smooth it out. Chill in the refrigerator.

Just before serving, sprinkle the top with brown sugar and torch the top, or place the whole cake under the hot broiler for a few minutes to make a candy crust. Watch carefully—either method will burn quickly!

Garnish with the blueberries and a spoonful of Ouzo Raisins beside each cake slice.

. . . .

Tip: Whip eggs and sugar over a double boiler long enough that the yellow of the eggs are slightly whipped and have turned into a light, creamy pastel color. This will give you maximum volume and help the sugar dissolve.

. . . .

Goat Cheese Brûlé Cake

Belgian Waffle Gratin
with Thyme-Infused Sugar Beet Syrup

A two-for-one special! Breakfast or dessert—take your pick.

Thyme-Infused Sugar Beet Syrup

3/4 cup sugar beet syrup or maple syrup
1 sprig thyme
6 Belgium waffles, store purchased
1 tbsp. unsalted butter, melted
8 oz. Oka cheese, grated
4 oz. Brie, rind removed, cut into cubes
2 pears, cored, thinly sliced
2 tsp. lemon zest, or zest from 1 medium lemon

Preheat the oven to 350°F.

In a small pot over medium heat, combine sugar beet syrup and thyme and simmer for 3 minutes. Remove the sprig of thyme and set aside. Keep syrup warm.

Brush the waffles with melted butter and place on a baking sheet. Spoon grated cheese onto the waffles, portion out the Brie, then bake for 3 minutes. Remove from the oven. Turn on the broiler and place the upper rack on the top position. Broil waffles until the cheese is bubbling and golden brown. Watch carefully so as not to burn.

To serve, place the waffles onto warmed plates, top with pear slices, and spoon on the warm syrup. Garnish with lemon zest and serve immediately.

. . . .

Tip: Sugar beet syrup is a unique cross between molasses and syrup. Sweet and sticky, yet a little bitter.

. . . .

The Sugar Rush

Because I wanted to be a great pastry chef, I would always offer to work extra hours in the bakery departments of the hotels where I worked in Europe. Although I am now a pro at finding my way around a pastry shop, I am still a rookie in the eyes of any bona fide pastry chef. This is because of the fact that I am a chef, and chefs don't know how to measure! We use our hands as scales and adjust everything from taste and seasonings to color, texture, and presentation as we go along. This is not to say that I haven't had some great successes pretending to be a pastry chef. And I have certainly managed to come up with my fair share of "Grand Finale Desserts."

Baking is a science that requires precise weights and measurements all the way down to the gram. In any restaurant kitchen there is an unspoken rule between the chef and the pastry chef that states, "This is my space and that is your space." The line of distinction may be invisible to outsiders but for those who work in the kitchen, it is more than obvious.

I was always told that a great dessert can take an average meal and turn it into a fantastic meal. The last dish you serve, the final taste your guests leave the table with, is what everyone remembers when they recall the dinner they had together.

These dessert recipes are old, unique German classics that have been transformed into refined, modern decadence. Of all the recipes in this book, these have the most truly old-world flavors. Here are some of my best attempts at crossing that invisible kitchen divide in order to create memorable last bites.

Desserts

Desserts

Nougat Mousse
with Rum Balls

I grew up with hazelnut spread on my bread instead of peanut

butter. Now that I am old enough to have rum, this treat keeps

me young at heart.

Nougat Mousse

3 gelatin sheets
1 egg
1 egg yolk
1/4 cup sugar
1/4 cup white chocolate, coarsely chopped
1 cup nougat hazelnut paste or hazelnut spread
2 oz. hazelnut liqueur
1 oz. rum
2 cups whipping cream, whipped

In a small bowl of cold water, soak gelatin sheets until they become soft and pliable.

In a double boiler, whisk the egg, egg yolk, and sugar until thick ribbons form.

Remove the gelatin sheets from the water and stir into the egg mixture.

Add the white chocolate pieces and whisk until melted.

Stir in the nougat, liqueur, and rum. Set aside until room temperature.

Fold in 1/4 of the whipped cream until it's completely incorporated then add the remaining whipped cream and repeat the same process.

Pour into individual glasses or dessert bowls and chill for 4 hours.

Rum Balls

1 lb. chocolate, coarsely chopped
1 lb. store-bought pound cake, cut into cubes
1 cup toasted ground almonds
1 tbsp. sugar
3 tbsp. cocoa powder
6 oz. rum
2 oz. crème de cacao
1 cup marzipan

In a medium pot over medium heat, melt the chocolate. Set aside for dipping.

In the bowl of an electric mixer, add the cake cubes, toasted ground almonds, sugar, and cocoa powder and stir until mixture has a dough-like consistency.

Add in the rum, crème de cacao, and the marzipan. Combine until a soft dough forms.

Using a small ice cream scoop or a heaping tablespoon, form into small golf balls and cool in the fridge to set the shape.

Dip the chilled balls into the melted chocolate then carefully scoop out with a fork and place on a tray lined with waxed paper or parchment paper. Chill. To serve, garnish the Nougat Mousse with Rum Balls.

Nougat Mousse with Rum Balls

Chocolate Soup

Nic Prong, a young head chef at my Ten Restaurant, came up

with this unbelievable bowl of gooey chocolate indulgence. I

hope you enjoy it.

2 cups whipping cream
2 cups skim milk
10 1/2 oz. 70% dark chocolate, chopped
2 oz. brandy
2 oz. Kahlúa
2 oz. crème de cacao
1 pound cake, store bought
1 oz. white chocolate shavings
1/4 cup whipping cream, whipped

In a double boiler, or metal bowl that fits over a pot of boiling water, place cream and milk; add dark chocolate. Stir until chocolate melts into a smooth mixture.

Add the liqueurs and cook until mixture begins to boil. Remove from heat and portion into individual serving bowls.

Refrigerate for a minimum of 2 hours.

To garnish, cut pound cake into croutons and toast in the oven. Top the soup with croutons, white chocolate shavings, and a dollop of whipped cream.

Semolina Mousse with Niagara Fruits

I had to make this dessert when I was a year and a half into my

apprenticeship, and I remember it just like it was yesterday.

5 gelatin sheets
2 cups whole milk
1/2 vanilla bean
2 tsp. lemon zest, or the zest from 1 lemon
2 tsp. orange zest, or the zest from 1 orange
pinch salt
1/3 cup semolina flour
3/4 cup sugar
2 eggs, separated
1 cup whipping cream

In a small bowl of cold water, soak gelatin sheets until they become soft and pliable.

In a medium pan, over medium heat, simmer the milk, vanilla bean, lemon zest, orange zest, and salt. Whisk in the semolina flour and continue to simmer for 7 minutes. Remove the pot from the heat and whisk in the softened gelatin sheets.

In a small bowl, whisk 1/4 cup of sugar and 2 egg yolks. Fold into the semolina mixture. Let cool to room temperature.

Whip 1/4 cup of sugar and 2 egg whites until peaks form. Fold into the semolina and egg yolk mixture.

Whip the cream and last 1/4 cup of sugar to hard peaks and fold into the mixture.

Pour into round molds, glasses, or bowls and refrigerate for at least 4 hours to set.

Niagara Fruits

Peaches: 2 peaches, juice of 1/2 lemon, 1/2 cup icing
    sugar, 1 oz. peach schnapps
Plums: 2 plums, juice of 1/2 lemon, 1/4 cup icing sugar,
    dash of cinnamon
Apples: 1 apple, peeled, cored, and sliced, juice of 1/2
    lemon, 1/2 cup icing sugar, 1/2 oz. brandy
Grapes: 1/4 lb. grapes, juice of 1/2 lemon, 1 tbsp. honey
Strawberries: 1 pint strawberries, 1/4 cup icing sugar,
    juice of 1/2 orange

For all these fruits, lightly toss and steep in the accent flavors.

To serve the mousse, set the mold in a bowl of hot water for just a few seconds then turn onto a serving plate.

Scatter the fruit around the mousse so the plate looks like a painter's palette.

One dessert, five flavor experiences.

. . . .

Tip: You can get through this recipe quite quickly by whipping the egg whites, then the cream with sugar, and have them sitting in the refrigerator ready to go.

. . . .

Semolina Mousse with Niagara Fruits

Tree Cake and Rum Berries

This cake is typical of a recipe that any apprentice pastry chef would have to make for a final test of skill. Why wait for school when you can put yourself to the test now?

Tree Cake

12 egg yolks
1 cup almond paste or marzipan
1 1/2 cups unsalted butter, melted
2 tbsp. corn syrup or glucose
2 tsp. lemon zest, or the zest from 1 lemon
1/2 scrapings from vanilla bean
pinch salt
1 oz. rum
16 egg whites
1 1/2 cups sugar
1 1/4 cup corn starch
1 1/4 cup pastry flour
icing sugar

Preheat oven to 450°F.

In a large mixing bowl, using an electric mixer, whip the egg yolks and almond paste until smooth.

Add the butter, corn syrup, lemon zest, vanilla bean scrapings, salt, and rum. Beat until frothy. Set aside.

In another large mixing bowl, using an electric mixer, whip the egg whites, sugar, and corn starch until stiff peaks form.

Carefully fold egg white mixture into egg yolk mixture, then fold in the flour.

In a nonstick 3-inch by 6-inch by 2-inch baking dish, ladle just enough batter to cover the bottom of the pan. Place under the broiler until batter is lightly browned. Remove from the oven and ladle in another layer, then place under the broiler. Repeat until all the batter is used. You should end up with 10 to 15 layers of cake, each the size of the baking dish.

When the cake has cooled and set, using a cookie cutter, cut out circle shapes and dust them with icing sugar.

Rum Berries

1 cup rum liqueur
3 tbsp. lemon juice, or the juice from 1 lemon
2 tsp. lemon zest, or the zest from 1 lemon
1/2 cup icing sugar
1 cup strawberries
1 cup blueberries
1 cup raspberries
1 cup blackberries

To a small pot over medium heat, add the rum, lemon juice, lemon zest, and icing sugar. Whisk together. When hot, pour over the berries, mix gently, and chill.

Chocolate Paté

1 1/2 cups 35% cream
2 oz. dark rum
4 oz. crème de cacao
2 cups semisweet chocolate pieces

In a small pot over medium heat, stir together cream, rum, and crème de cacao.

When mixture is warm, whisk in the chocolate pieces; stir until chocolate is melted.

Cool to room temperature.

Plate the pieces of cake, then place a dollop of Chocolate Paté on each piece. Spoon the Rum Berries onto the side of the plate.

Tip: To whip egg whites, you need a very clean bowl. Start by whipping the egg whites first, then the yolks—this way you don't have to clean the mixer bowl.

Tree Cake and Rum Berries

Marzipan Poppy Seed Bundt Cake with Wild Blueberry Compote

Until now, marzipan has always been the special-occasion ingredient. I've added some poppy seeds and a cake recipe that will soak up the wild blueberry sauce. Trust me, a special occasion is about to happen.

Marzipan Poppy Seed Bundt Cake

5 egg yolks
3/4 cup sugar
1/2 cup marzipan
1 tsp. cinnamon
5 egg whites
1/2 cup whole wheat flour
1/2 cup cake flour
1/4 tsp. salt
1 cup poppy seeds
1/3 cup ground almonds
3 tbsp. lemon juice, or the juice from 1 lemon
2 tsp. lemon zest, or the zest from 1 lemon
icing sugar, for dusting

Preheat oven to 350°F.

Lightly butter a Bundt cake pan, then dust with flour.

In a large bowl, whisk egg yolks and 1/2 cup sugar together until sugar is dissolved and mixture is frothy. Stir in the marzipan and cinnamon.

In a separate bowl, whisk the egg whites and remaining sugar until firm peaks form.

In a third bowl, sift together whole wheat flour, cake flour, salt, poppy seeds, and ground almonds. Fold in egg yolk mixture. When completely mixed, fold in the egg whites, then the lemon juice and zest.

Pour into Bundt cake pan and bake for 25 minutes, or until a toothpick comes out clean.

When cool, dust with icing sugar.

Wild Blueberry Compote

1/2 cup icing sugar
2 tbsp. lemon juice, or the juice from 1 lemon
1 cup blueberry juice
2 cups wild local blueberries

In a small pot over medium heat, combine icing sugar, lemon juice, and blueberry juice. Simmer for 10 minutes or until you have a syrup-like consistency.

Add in the blueberries and bring to a simmer then remove from the heat. Place in a bowl, cover with plastic wrap, and chill.

Cut a slice of Poppy Seed Cake and serve with the Wild Blueberry Compote on the side.

Chocolate Sauerkraut Cake with Boozy Cherries

This recipe is my own leap of faith. I've combined chocolate and sauerkraut to make a cake for any adventurous soul ready to think outside the box and try different things.

Cake

1 cup butter
1 1/2 cups brown sugar
2 eggs
1 1/2 cups flour
6 tbsp. cocoa powder
1 1/2 tsp. baking soda
1/4 tsp. salt
2/3 cup sour cream
1 tsp. vanilla
3/4 cup hot coffee
3/4 cup drained sauerkraut, very finely chopped

Preheat the oven to 350°F.

Grease and flour a 14-inch by 10-inch by 1-inch pan.

In a mixing bowl, using an electric mixer, cream butter and sugar until light and fluffy. Add the eggs one at a time.

In a separate bowl, sift together dry ingredients.

Stir the dry ingredients into the egg butter mixture, alternating in two parts with sour cream. Mix in the vanilla.

Gradually add hot coffee (batter will be thin). Stir in the sauerkraut.

Bake 55 minutes or until toothpick is dry to the touch.

Stout Ganache

1/2 cup whipping cream
1/2 cup stout beer
1 cup semisweet chocolate, coarsely chopped

In small pot over medium heat, stir together cream and beer and simmer for 3 minutes.

Whisk in the chocolate pieces until melted.

Remove from the heat and cool until you have a thick syrup-like consistency.

Pour over the cooled cake and let it run down the sides.

Boozy Cherries

1/2 cup sugar
1 stick cinnamon
1 cup cherry juice
1/2 cup corn syrup
1/4 cup rum
1 cup red wine
1 tbsp. amaretto liqueur
1 large orange, juiced
2 cups black cherries

In a small pot over medium heat, combine all the ingredients except cherries.

Reduce the liquid by 75% or until you have a syrup-like consistency.

Fold in the cherries and cool. Serve on the plate beside cake.

Butter Cake with Roasted Rhubarb and Strawberries

This wicked delight of a recipe is a definite one up on Grandma's nice little cake. Eat it with this in mind: There may be lots of butter in this recipe, but my Oma is still baking this cake and still going strong.

Cake Dough

1 tbsp. dry yeast
1 cup milk, warmed
pinch sugar
2 cups cake flour
1/2 cup unsalted butter, melted
1/4 tsp. salt
2 tsp. lemon zest, or the zest from 1 lemon

Preheat the oven to 350°F.

Line an 18-inch by 12-inch by 1-inch baking tray with parchment paper.

In a small bowl, stir together yeast, warm milk, and a pinch of sugar. Set aside.

In a large bowl, combine the flour, butter, salt, and lemon zest.

When the yeast is frothy, slowly pour it into the flour; mix with your hands until a soft, smooth dough forms. Cover the bowl with a clean cloth and place in a warm place to rise

When the dough has risen to twice its size, punch it down and carefully stretch it so it completely covers the baking sheet.

Cover with a cloth and, again, let is rise in a warm place for approximately 30 minutes.

After it has risen to double its size, use your finger to put indents in the dough every couple of inches. Don't press all the way through the dough.

Topping

3/4 cup unsalted butter
1/2 cup sugar
3/4 cup sliced almonds
1/2 cup icing sugar

Place 1/8 teaspoon of butter into each indent, then sprinkle the whole surface of the dough with half the sugar. Bake for 15 minutes.

Sprinkle on the slices of almonds and the rest of the sugar. Return to the oven and bake for an additional 5 minutes. The cake is done when a toothpick comes out clean.

Roasted Rhubarb and Strawberries

1 cup rhubarb, peeled and cut into large dice
1 cup whole strawberries, hulled and halved
1 vanilla bean, scrapings
2 tbsp. olive oil
1/4 tsp. white pepper
2 tbsp. lemon juice, or the juice from 1 lemon
2 tbsp. honey
icing sugar, for dusting

In a large bowl, stir together rhubarb, strawberries, vanilla bean scrapings, olive oil, and pepper. Spread coated fruit out on a baking sheet and roast for 15 minutes.

Place the roasted fruits into a bowl and add the lemon juice and honey.

Assembly

Cut the cake into triangular pieces and dust with icing sugar.

To serve, add a spoonful of the roasted fruits just to the side of each piece of cake.

No Campfire S'mores

Who among you hasn't sat at a campfire and cooked S'mores over an open flame? Forget lugging logs and watching your marshmallows burn. Here's a way to stay warm and dry and still lick chocolate from your fingers.

Chocolate Crumble

1/2 cup white chocolate, cut into pieces
1 tbsp. white sugar
1 tbsp. brown sugar

Preheat the oven to 350°F.

Place the chocolate pieces on a baking sheet lined with a non-stick baking sheet pad and bake for 4 to 7 minutes, or until chocolate is golden brown. Watch carefully: chocolate can burn very quickly. Remove from oven; allow to cool and set.

Break the chocolate into crumbles.

Combine the white and brown sugars and toss with the crumbled chocolate.

Marshmallows

4 gelatin sheets
1/4 cup water
1 3/4 cups sugar
3/4 cup English syrup or corn syrup
1 tsp. vanilla extract
1/4 tsp. salt
icing sugar, for dusting

In a small bowl of cold water, soak the gelatin sheets until they become soft and pliable.

In a medium pot over medium-high heat, add the water, sugar, and syrup and bring to a boil.

Pour sugar mixture into the bowl of an electric mixer. Take the gelatin sheets out of the water and add to the bowl. Whip on high for 10 minutes, or until light and fluffy.

Add the vanilla and salt and whip for one minute.

Line a 9-inch by 9-inch by 2-inch tray with oil and pour in the marshmallow mixture. Cover with parchment paper or waxed paper, then refrigerate for 3 hours.

Preheat the broiler.

Dust a cutting board with icing sugar, turn out the cooled marshmallow sheet onto the board, and cut into the shapes of your choice.

Place the cut shapes on a baking sheet lined with parchment paper and quickly toast the marshmallows. Don't take your eyes off them—just like over a campfire, they will burn quickly.

Chocolate Paté

1 1/2 cups whipping cream
2 cups semisweet chocolate
4 oz. crème de cacao
2 oz. dark rum
8 graham crackers

In a small pot over medium heat, simmer the cream until very warm, but not boiling. Whisk in chocolate, liqueur, and rum. Set aside and allow mixture to set to a peanut-butter-like consistency, then spoon generously onto 4 graham crackers. Top each with another graham cracker. Set aside.

Spun Sugar Cage

3 cups sugar
2 cups water

Take 2 dinner forks and tape them together with prongs facing outwards.

In a small pot over medium-high heat, simmer the sugar and water until mixture has caramelized and temperature reaches 223 to 225°F on a candy thermometer.

On a tabletop, over a 2-foot-long sheet of parchment paper, dip the forks into the hot sugar and pull quickly straight over the paper to form approximately 12-inch-long threads of gold. Keep adding hot sugar to the forks and run back and forth to make a mound of about 12 to 15 threads. While threads are still warm, cut into quarters giving you four strips. Roll into a cone shape. Put the 4 cones aside to set.

Hold the cone in one hand and place the chocolate-smothered graham crackers inside, add toasted marshmallows, and top with Chocolate Crumble.

No Campfire S'mores

Kitchen Basics

Kitchen Basics

I work hard to cultivate an atmosphere of quality and excellence in all my kitchens. The standard dishes of my kitchens, like ground rules, give my chefs a foundation to work from. I hope the standards can do the same for you. Here is a compilation of basic recipes used in my kitchens. The great thing about these recipes is that you can stick with them as is or get creative by incorporating them into your own ideas.

Kitchen Basics

Kitchen Basics

Vegetable Stock

I call this my "vegetable tea." Loaded with tons of flavor from the tomato, fennel, and herbs, this broth is not only tasty but ultra good for you. Use in any recipes calling for vegetable stock.

2 carrots, diced
3 onions, diced
3 fennel bulbs, diced
1 leek, white only, sliced
2 vine-ripened tomatoes, diced
1 clove garlic, sliced
1 cup olive oil
2 quarts cold water
3 quarts ice cubes
1 cup parsley leaves
1 cup basil leaves
1 tbsp. thyme
1 tbsp. cracked black peppercorns
1 bay leaf
1 tbsp. salt
1 tsp. celery salt

In a stockpot or other large, heavy-bottomed pot on high heat, sauté the vegetables and garlic in oil for about 10 minutes or until onion and leek are translucent. Add the cold water and ice cubes and reduce the temperature to medium. Simmer, uncovered, for 2 hours. During the last half hour, add the herbs and seasonings. Using a ladle, transfer the broth into a clean container. To prevent bacteria from forming, chill the stock quickly by sealing it and placing it in a larger container of ice cubes.

· ·

Tip: Adding the ice cubes as the broth is simmering prolongs the flavor extraction time and keeps the broth clear by weighing down any unwanted particles.

· ·

Sweet Orange Sauce

This is a great addition to any poultry, veal, or pork dish.

2 tbsp. oil
1 onion, diced
1 star anise, sliced
3 seedless unpeeled oranges, diced
2 cups red wine
2 cups chicken stock
2 cups orange juice
1/8 tsp. grated ginger root
3 tbsp. brown sugar
2 tbsp. balsamic vinegar
salt and white pepper to taste
4 oz. orange liqueur

In a small pot, heat the oil, then add the onion, star anise, and oranges. Deglaze with the red wine, simmer, and reduce by 80%. Add the stock, orange juice, and ginger. Simmer 10 minutes. Add the brown sugar, balsamic vinegar, salt, and pepper. Strain into a clean pot using a fine sieve. Bring the sauce to a simmer and whisk in the orange liqueur. Taste and adjust the seasoning if necessary.

Port Wine Reduction

Next time you cook a cheese, beef, or pork dish, you must

make this reduction as a flavor booster.

1 tbsp. olive oil
1 cup minced shallots
1 tsp. thyme, chopped
1/4 cup sugar
1 tsp. cracked peppercorns
1 bottle ruby port wine

In a small pot over medium heat, add the olive oil and sauté the shallots, thyme, sugar, and peppercorns until lightly golden browned. Deglaze with the port and reduce by 90%. Strain through a fine mesh sieve and set aside or store until ready to use.

BBQ Sauce

1/4 cup ground cumin
1/2 cup ancho chili powder
3 cups brown sugar
2 cups white vinegar
3 cups molasses
1/2 cup Worcestershire sauce
4 tbsp. salt
1/2 tsp. liquid smoke
8 cups ketchup
8 cups chicken broth
1/2 cup corn starch
1/2 cup water

In a medium pot over medium-high heat, toast the chili powder and ground cumin. Add the brown sugar and stir until sugar has melted.

Add the vinegar, molasses, Worcestershire sauce, salt, liquid smoke, ketchup, and chicken broth. Reduce heat to medium-low and simmer for 30 minutes.

In a small bowl, combine the corn starch and water then add to the simmering sauce, stirring occasionally. Continue for 20 minutes or until the sauce has thickened, on a low heat and watch to make sure it doesn't stick to the bottom and burn.

Olaf's Black Spice Rub

A must-have during the barbecue season.

3 cups vegetable oil
6 cloves garlic
1 cup coriander
2 cups scallions
1/2 cup red pepper
1 tbsp. thyme, chopped
1 Scotch bonnet
4 1/2 tbsp. lime juice, or the juice from 3 limes
2 tbsp. allspice
1 tsp. brown sugar
1 tbsp. molasses
1/4 tsp. nutmeg
1/4 tsp. cinnamon
1 tbsp. salt

Place all ingredients into a food processor or blender and purée until smooth.

. . . .

Tip: This is a very versatile rub. It can be used with pork, chicken, shellfish, and fish. Store in an airtight container. Keeps up to 2 weeks in the fridge.

. . . .

Braised Duck Leg

Used in Mini Duck Burgers, Duck Ravioli, Chicken Stuffed with

Orange Braised Duck, and Duck Empanadas.

8 duckling quarters (leg with thigh attached)
1/3 cup vegetable oil
1 carrot, diced
2 celery stalks, diced
1 onion, diced
2 parsnips, diced
3 cups red wine
4 cups chicken stock
2 bay leaves
1 sprig rosemary, chopped
1 sprig thyme, chopped
6 tbsp. orange juice, or the juice of 2 oranges
4 tsp. orange zest, or the zest of 2 oranges
3 tbsp. lemon juice, or the juice of 1 lemon
2 tsp. lemon zest, or the zest of 1 lemon
salt and white pepper

Preheat the oven to 350F°.

Using a sharp knife, score the duck skin in a checkerboard pattern. You will need a large, deep oven pan with a removable rack. Remove the rack and place the pan on the stove over high heat. Sear duck legs in the oil until well browned.

Remove the duck legs from the pan and add the vegetables. Sauté, then deglaze with the wine and simmer for 10 minutes.

Add the chicken stock, bay leaves, herbs, citrus juices, and zests.

Set the rack on top of the vegetables and place the duck meat on the rack. Season well with salt and pepper. Cover the pan with parchment paper and foil. Bake for 50 minutes.

Remove the foil and parchment paper and continue cooking for 15 to 20 more minutes, or until the meat falls off the bones. Remove from the oven and let cool. Once cool enough to handle, flake the meat off the bones. Pour the vegetables and pan juices into a fine sieve and strain into a bowl.

Store the meat in the strained juices for 1 to 2 days in the refrigerator.

Basic Spaetzle

5 eggs
3/4 cup water
4 cups all-purpose flour
1 tbsp. oil
1 tsp. salt
1/2 tsp. white pepper

Using an electric mixer with a dough paddle attachment, combine eggs and water in a medium bowl then add all remaining ingredients. Mix for 10 minutes, or until the mixture begins to form long, stringy strands. If the mixture is too doughy, add a teaspoon of water and continue mixing until the desired elasticity is achieved. Form into a ball, wrap in plastic wrap, and refrigerate for at least 30 minutes.

Pass the dough through a spaetzle press into a large pot of boiling salted water.

The spaetzle is ready when it floats to the surface. Use a slotted spoon to transfer the spaetzle to a strainer.

Serve warm or refrigerate in an airtight container until needed.

Whole Wheat Spaetzle

2 1/2 cups whole wheat flour
1 1/2 cups all-purpose flour
1 tsp. salt
1/2 tsp. white pepper
5 eggs
3/4 cup milk

Using an electric mixer with the dough paddle attachment, combine the flours, salt, and pepper on low speed. Add the eggs one at a time then gradually add the milk to form a wet dough. Allow the dough to knead in the mixer for about 10 minutes. Wrap in plastic wrap and refrigerate for 30 minutes.

Press the dough through a spaetzle press into a large pot of salted boiling water. When the noodles float, they are ready. Use a slotted spoon and transfer the spaetzle to a strainer.

Serve warm or refrigerate in an airtight container until needed.

Red Beet Spaetzle

3 red beets, medium size
1 tbsp. sugar
1 tsp. salt
3/4 cup water
1 tbsp. oil
5 cups flour
1 tsp. salt
1/2 tsp. white pepper
5 eggs
1 tbsp. oil

Peel the beets and cut into large pieces. Bring a pot of water to boil. Add sugar and salt and cook the beets until tender. Let them cool slightly, then purée in the blender.

In an electric mixer with the dough paddle attachment on low speed, combine the red beet purée, water, and oil, then add the flour, pepper, and salt. Once the flour is mixed in, add the eggs one at a time. When you have a wet dough, knead in the mixer for about 10 minutes. Refrigerate for 30 minutes.

Press the dough through a spaetzle press into a large pot of boiling salted water. When the noodles float to the surface, they are ready. Use a slotted spoon to transfer the spaetzle to a strainer.

Serve warm, or refrigerate in an airtight container until needed.

Basic Risotto

2 tbsp. olive oil
1 onion, finely diced
1 cup arborio rice
3/4 cup white wine
4 cups vegetable or chicken stock
1/3 cup unsalted butter
1/3 cup Parmesan cheese
salt and white pepper to taste

In a large pot, heat the olive oil and sauté the onions until translucent. Add the rice and quickly sauté. Deglaze with the white wine and cook for 3 to 5 minutes until liquid is reduced by 90%.

Stir in 1 cup of stock. Continue stirring until all the stock has been absorbed, approximately 3 to 5 minutes, then add another cup of stock.

Keep adding and stirring stock, one cup at a time, until it has all been used. The rice should end up soft but still *al dente*.

Add the butter and cheese. Taste and season with salt and pepper.

Serve immediately.

Basic Ravioli

1/3 cup milk
1/3 cup vegetable oil
6 eggs
3 1/2 cups flour

Egg Wash

1 large egg
1/2 cup milk

Combine the milk, oil, and eggs in a bowl, preferably one with a spout.

Place the flour into a mixer with the dough paddle attachment.

Pour the milk mixture into the flour until you get a soft, completely mixed dough ball. Wrap the dough in plastic wrap and chill for 30 minutes.

Whisk the egg and milk together and set aside for an egg wash.

Following the directions for your pasta machine, roll the dough out gradually from thick to thin. A rolling pin can be used to do this but it will take longer. Either way the dough should end up about 1/16 of an inch in thickness.

Cut the ravioli dough into 4-inch squares. You will need 8 squares in total. Make a mound of about 2 tbsp. of the stuffing mixture in the center of the ravioli squares. Make an egg wash with the egg and milk and cover the perimeter of the squares. Cover with another sheet of ravioli dough and remove any air pockets. Seal firmly with a scalloped pastry roller or your fingers. When ready to serve, blanch the ravioli in boiling salted water for 3 minutes until tender.

Strudel Dough

Makes enough dough for one 3-foot-long log of strudel.

1 1/3 cup flour
2 tsp. salt
2/3 cup warm water
1/4 cup vegetable oil
melted butter

Preheat oven to 350°F.

In a bowl, combine the flour and salt and make a well in the middle. Using your hands, carefully work in the water and oil to form a soft dough. Let rest for 30 minutes.

Cover a table or other large surface with a clean tablecloth. Sprinkle the tablecloth with flour, then roll the dough out to 1/4-inch thickness. Circling your way around the table, evenly stretch the dough until paper-thin. This part is much easier if you have someone to help. Continue to stretch the dough until you cover a 2 x 3 foot surface. Butter the top of the dough and mound filling of choice (apples, pears, mushrooms, fish, chicken) across the bottom length. Using the ends of the tablecloth, fold dough over filling lengthwise and roll the entire length of the folded strudel into a cylinder. Twist the strudel every twelve inches, like sausage links and place on a parchment paper lined baking sheet. Brush the tops with melted butter and bake for 15 minutes.

Flatbread

2 cups flour
1 tsp. sugar
1/2 tsp. salt
4 egg whites
1 tbsp. olive oil
1/2 cup warm water

Egg wash

1 egg
1/2 cup milk

Topping

4 cloves garlic, sliced
1 tbsp. coarsely chopped pine nuts
1 tsp. sea salt
2 tbsp. rosemary, chopped
1 tsp. fennel seeds

Preheat the oven to 400°F.

Using a mixer with a dough paddle, mix the flour, sugar, and salt.

In a separate bowl, combine the egg whites, olive oil, and warm water.

Slowly mix into the flour mixture. Wrap the dough in plastic wrap and let it rest in the refrigerator for 30 minutes.

Roll out to 1/8 inch and cut into shapes of choice: triangles, rectangles, and so on. Place on a parchment paper-lined baking sheet. Brush with egg wash and sprinkle with topping. Bake 8 minutes.

• •

Tip: For a rustic look, bake the rolled-out dough in one large sheet, then break into large pieces and serve in a breadbasket.

• •

Blender Dressings and Vinaigrettes

Blender Dressings and Vinaigrettes

Learning to master salads is one of the first tasks to be assigned in any professional kitchen. And, of course, the art of salad is not complete without dressings and vinaigrettes. I believe salads and dressing that are prepared in restaurants have a certain mystique. In fact, most of the requests I get for recipes come from people wanting to know about salads and dressings. I think one of the key components to the success of dressings is making them in large batches—they always seem to taste better this way. Here are a few basic tips and a couple of creative ideas for dressings and vinaigrettes.

Blender Dressings and Vinaigrettes

Blender Dressings and Vinaigrettes

Key Components of Dressings and Vinaigrettes

Acids: flavored vinegars, citrus juices, sour fruit sauces
Textures: fruit and vegetable pulps, herbs, mustards, syrups
Oils: flavored oils, corn or vegetable oils, nut oils, olive oils
Lighteners: mineral waters, stocks, broths

Rule of thumb: 1 part acid to 3 or 4 parts textures, oils, lighteners

Tools: large measuring cup, hand blender, food processor or blender

Seasoning: always season to taste. Taste dressings by dipping fresh greens into them. This will give you the truest representation of their flavors.

Citrus Vinaigrette

The acids from the fresh citrus juices are a great way to begin any menu because they wake up the appetite and get the digestive system going.

2 cups orange juice
3/4 cup lemon juice, or the juice from 4 lemons
2 tbsp. lime juice, or the juice from 3 limes
2 cups white wine vinegar
1/4 cup liquid honey
2 cups vegetable stock or water
2 cups vegetable oil
salt and white pepper to taste

Place all ingredients into a food processor or blender and purée for 2 minutes. Stop to adjust seasonings then blend for 30 seconds more. This dressing will keep in the refrigerator for up to 7 days. Blend or whisk before each use.

• •

Tip: I use real lemons and limes for this recipe. Lemons and limes produce more juice if they are at room temperature. If your fruit is cold, microwave it for a few seconds, then roll it on the counter with the palm of your hand before juicing. You will notice a big difference.

• •

Red Wine Vinaigrette

1/4 cup olive oil
1 medium red onion, minced
1 tsp. lemon zest, or the zest from half a lemon
1 cup red wine
1 tsp. oregano, chopped
1 tsp. thyme, chopped
1 tbsp. Dijon mustard
1/2 cup red wine vinegar
1 cup water
1/2 cup olive oil
sea salt
ground pepper

In a medium pot over medium high heat, heat 1/4 cup olive oil. Add red onion and lemon zest and sauté until onion is translucent. Deglaze with red wine, then add the oregano and thyme. Reduce liquid by 90% or until cooked down to a syrup. Allow to cool to room temperature. Let cool slightly.

Pour syrup into a blender, add the mustard, and purée. Season with salt and pepper then add the red wine vinegar. With blender still running, drizzle in the water and 1/2 cup olive oil.

Pass the blended dressing through a fine sieve and adjust salt and pepper to taste.

Wheat Germ Dressing

1/4 cup wheat germ, cracked
1/4 cup spelt
1 tbsp. minced shallot
1 cup chamomile tea, steeped and hot
1/2 bulb fennel, diced
2 cups cucumber juice
4 cups yogurt
2 tbsp. lemon juice, or the juice from 1 lemon
2 tsp. lemon zest, or the zest from 1 lemon
1/2 cup herbal vinegar
1 cup oil
salt and pepper to taste

In a large bowl, combine wheat germ, spelt, and shallots. Cover with the hot tea and let sit until room temperature.

In a food processor, purée the tea mixture then add all remaining ingredients except oil, salt, and pepper. Purée again, then add the oil in a slow drizzle while still processing. Season with salt and pepper.

. . . .

Tip: The hot tea wilts the shallots and softens the spelt and wheat germ.

. . . .

White Raisin, Cauliflower, and Caper Dressing

You'll need to make a batch of the Vegetable Stock on page 182.

1 head cauliflower, cut into florets
3/4 cup olive oil
salt and pepper to taste
8 shallots, sliced
1 cup sugar
1 cup white wine vinegar
1/2 cup white raisins
1 cup capers
6 cups Vegetable Stock (page 182)
2 cups cauliflower juice
3 tbsp. lemon juice, or the juice and zest from 1 lemon
1/4 cup parsley, sliced
1/2 tsp. nutmeg

Preheat oven to 350°F.

Toss the cauliflower florets in 2 tbsp. of oil until coated, season with salt and pepper, then place in a baking dish and roast for 30 minutes.

In a medium pot, over medium heat, sauté the shallots in 1 tbsp. olive oil until light brown. Add the sugar and vinegar and simmer until you have a syrup-like consistency.

Add the raisins, capers, roasted cauliflower, and vegetable stock. Simmer for 5 minutes, then let cool.

Transfer to a food processor or blender and purée until smooth.

Whisk in the cauliflower juice, the remaining olive oil, lemon juice, zest, and parsley. Taste and, if necessary, season with nutmeg; adjust salt and pepper.

. . . .

Tip: Keep this mixture chunky, and it will make a great relish or sauce for fish or shellfish.

. . . .

Too-Good-for-You Salad with Wheat Germ Dressing

Index

On the Curve Hot Stove & Wine Bar

TEN Restaurant & Wine Bar

West 50 Pourhouse & Grille